SPECTRUM®

Math

Grade 2

Published by Spectrum®
an imprint of Carson-Dellosa Publishing LLC
Greensboro, NC

Spectrum®
An imprint of Carson-Dellosa Publishing LLC
P.O. Box 35665
Greensboro, NC 27425 USA

ISBN 978-1-4838-0870-3

01-099187784

Table of Contents Grade 2

Table of Contents, continued

Check What You Learned

SHOW YOUR WORK

Adding and Subtracting 2-Digit Numbers (With Renaming)

Solve each problem.

Yumi picks 50 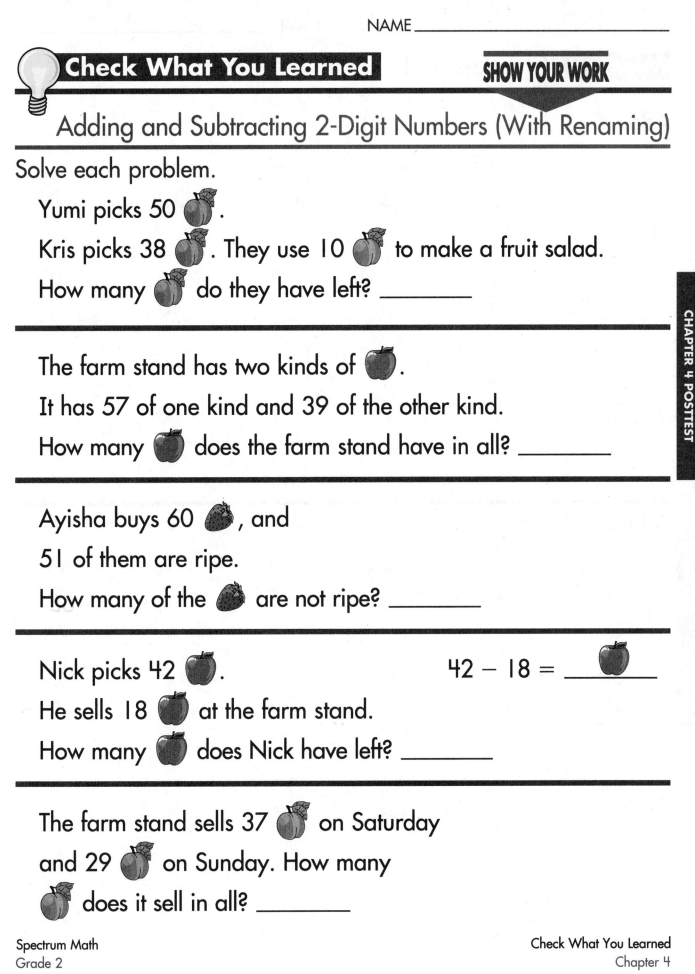.

Kris picks 38 . They use 10 to make a fruit salad.

How many do they have left? _____

The farm stand has two kinds of .

It has 57 of one kind and 39 of the other kind.

How many does the farm stand have in all? _____

Ayisha buys 60 , and

51 of them are ripe.

How many of the are not ripe? _____

Nick picks 42 .

He sells 18 at the farm stand.

How many does Nick have left? _____

$42 - 18 =$ _____

The farm stand sells 37 on Saturday

and 29 on Sunday. How many

does it sell in all? _____

Mid-Test Chapters 1–4

Add.

4 +9	28 +15	44 + 5	8 +6	55 +39	1 +8

8 +9	63 +15	73 + 8	0 +5	23 +46	2 +6

12 23 + 4	30 17 +31	1 +3	4 +8	18 +34	48 +20

Subtract.

79 −43	7 −2	18 − 9	43 −15	12 − 3	68 −15

30 −19	15 − 8	10 − 3	46 −36	3 −0	43 − 6

14 − 6	8 −8	56 −44	72 −35	17 − 9	9 −4

Mid-Test Chapters 1–4

Odd or even? _____

Odd or even? _____

Count by 5. Start at 40.

40,   45,   ____,   ____,   60,   ____

Count by 2. Start at 12¢.

12¢, ____¢, ____¢, 18¢, ____¢, ____¢

Write an equation to match each array.

____ + ____ + ____ = ____

____ + ____ = ____

Mid-Test Chapters 1–4

Write an equation to match the array.

___ + ___ + ___ = ___

Count by 10.

40, ___, ___, ___, 80, 90, ___, ___, ___, ___, 140

Tell how many. Label odd or even. Write an equation that adds together two equal parts.

How many 🐟 ? _____

Odd or even? _____

___ + ___ = ___

SHOW YOUR WORK

Solve each problem.

Pascal picks 14 🌼 .

Kim picks 13 🌼 .

How many 🌼 do they pick in all? _____

The Williams family has 34 stuffed animals.

9 of them are 🧸 .

How many of them are not 🧸 ? _____

Mid-Test Chapters 1–4

Solve each problem.

Emil lends 3 📕 to Jeff.

He now has 12 📕 left.

How many 📕 did Emil start with? _____

Terrence has 24 📕.

Bella has 22 📕. Mike has 21 📕.

How many 📕 do they have in all? _____

An apple costs 🪙🪙.

An orange costs 🪙🪙🪙🪙🪙🪙.

How much do they cost? _____¢

The earth club plants 14 🌳 on Saturday

and 18 🌳 on Sunday.

How many 🌳 do they plant in all? _____

The earth club plants 45 🌼.

24 of the 🌼 are red. 13 of the 🌼 are yellow.

How many 🌼 are not red or yellow? _____

Check What You Know

Working with 3-Digit Numbers

Count by 5.

450, __455__, __460__, 465, 470, __475__, 480, __485__

Count by 10.

360, __370__, __380__, 390, 400, __410__, __420__, 430

Count by 100.

__100__, 200, __300__, __400__, 500, __600__, __700__

Write the number and its expanded form or number name.

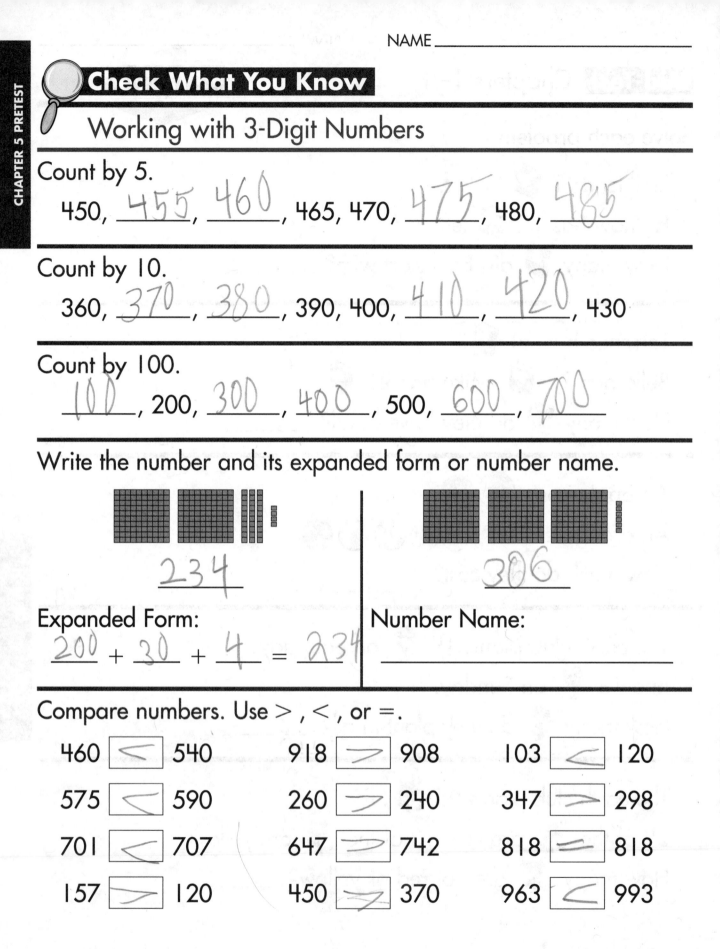

__234__   __306__

Expanded Form: Number Name:

__200__ + __30__ + __4__ = __234__   _____

Compare numbers. Use > , < , or =.

460	<	540	918	>	908	103	<	120
575	<	590	260	>	240	347	>	298
701	<	707	647	<	742	818	=	818
157	>	120	450	>	370	963	<	993

Lesson 5.7 Subtracting 2 Digits from 3 Digits

Rename 5 tens and 3 ones as 4 tens and 13 ones.		Subtract the ones. ↓	Rename 1 hundred and 4 tens as 14 tens.	Subtract the tens. ↓	
1 5 3 – 6 5	⁴¹³ 1 5̶3̶ – 6 5	⁴¹³ 1 5̶3̶ – 6 5 8	¹⁴¹³ 1̶ 5̶3̶ – 6 5 8	¹⁴¹³ 1̶ 5̶3̶ – 6 5 8 8	minuend subtrahend difference

Subtract.

1 6 2 – 7 3 8 9	1 7 5 – 9 7	1 8 2 – 9 4	1 0 3 – 1 7	1 1 6 – 3 9
1 7 4 – 9 5	1 4 7 – 6 8	1 3 2 – 6 5	1 1 5 – 4 9	1 0 7 – 3 9
1 0 1 – 7 5	1 0 0 – 9 2	1 2 7 – 7 9	1 3 3 – 4 4	1 4 2 – 7 3
1 4 1 – 6 3	1 3 7 – 7 9	1 4 2 – 7 3	1 5 3 – 6 7	1 5 5 – 9 6
1 0 0 – 7 2	1 0 6 – 4 8	1 1 7 – 8 8	1 2 4 – 6 6	1 6 3 – 8 9
1 7 2 – 8 7	1 6 1 – 9 2	1 4 5 – 6 6	1 3 2 – 5 7	1 3 0 – 4 3

Lesson 5.7 Subtracting 2 Digits from 3 Digits

Subtract.

132 − 71	196 − 87	165 − 59	163 − 71	119 − 29
106 − 51	100 − 29	153 − 69	147 − 88	192 − 75
175 − 95	169 − 99	142 − 37	140 − 93	131 − 57
167 − 76	173 − 82	192 − 95	143 − 77	126 − 54
117 − 26	100 − 33	175 − 46	142 − 57	136 − 47
176 − 89	143 − 54	140 − 39	173 − 75	163 − 92

Lesson 5.7 Subtracting 2 Digits from 3 Digits

Subtract.

144 − 86	122 − 31	191 − 75	175 − 93	144 − 65
121 − 37	106 − 42	165 − 43	162 − 47	181 − 57
106 − 99	127 − 49	136 − 58	124 − 75	143 − 52
685 − 96	444 − 67	612 − 22	786 − 19	950 − 99
865 − 92	710 − 7	475 − 89	627 − 10	751 − 93
509 − 75	696 − 5	815 − 25	545 − 57	115 − 72

Lesson 5.8 Adding 3-Digit Numbers

	Add the ones.	Add the tens.	Add the hundreds.
755 +469	755 +469 —— 4	755 +469 —— 24	755 + 469 —— 1224

Add.

123 +562 —— 685	982 +171	342 +591	782 +341	123 +321
862 +313	900 +130	720 +850	931 +111	823 +457
861 +421	862 +139	431 +250	782 +191	751 +605
791 +191	144 +800	192 +175	257 +147	203 +211
705 +719	641 +209	873 +505	700 +650	105 +341
593 +741	861 +209	735 +145	820 +431	738 +387

Lesson 5.9 Subtracting 3-Digit Numbers

Rename 2 tens and 1 one as 1 ten and 11 ones. Then, subtract the ones.

Rename 6 hundreds and 1 ten as 5 hundreds and 11 tens. Then, subtract the tens.

Subtract the hundreds.

```
  6 2 1        6 2 1        6 2 1        6 2 1   minuend
- 2 5 9      - 2 5 9      - 2 5 9      - 2 5 9   subtrahend
                    2           6 2        3 6 2  difference
```

Subtract.

```
  3 2 1        7 4 5        6 3 9        8 3 0        6 2 6
- 1 0 9      - 1 5 2      - 1 5 0      - 7 1 0      - 1 4 6
  2 1 2
```

```
  7 2 9        6 5 7        3 8 6        4 1 1        4 8 6
- 3 2 1      - 4 5 1      - 1 0 7      - 3 0 5      - 1 0 9
```

```
  9 8 3        9 7 1        8 7 6        5 4 9        7 2 1
- 6 5 2      - 5 7 2      - 3 5 7      - 3 6 0      - 1 4 4
```

```
  2 5 6        3 4 7        7 2 5        8 6 3        9 8 0
- 1 4 2      - 1 3 9      - 1 9 6      - 6 9 2      - 5 3 2
```

```
  5 4 3        7 6 2        1 3 2        9 2 1        6 3 1
- 4 5 7      - 1 3 5      - 1 0 7      - 5 7 1      - 5 4 5
```

```
  5 3 1        7 2 0        5 8 2        7 9 3        6 1 2
- 2 5 0      - 3 7 1      - 3 5 7      - 4 5 7      - 4 8 3
```

Lesson 5.10 Checking Addition with Subtraction

To check

215 + 109 = 324,

subtract 109 from 324.

$$
\begin{array}{r}
215 \\
+109 \\
\hline
324 \\
-109 \\
\hline
215
\end{array}
$$

These should be the same.

Add. Check each answer.

$$
\begin{array}{r}
157 \\
+212 \\
\hline
369 \\
-212 \\
\hline
157
\end{array}
\qquad
\begin{array}{r}
719 \\
+182 \\
\hline
\end{array}
\qquad
\begin{array}{r}
312 \\
+105 \\
\hline
\end{array}
\qquad
\begin{array}{r}
213 \\
+519 \\
\hline
\end{array}
\qquad
\begin{array}{r}
306 \\
+215 \\
\hline
\end{array}
$$

$$
\begin{array}{r}
710 \\
+398 \\
\hline
\end{array}
\qquad
\begin{array}{r}
357 \\
+249 \\
\hline
\end{array}
\qquad
\begin{array}{r}
712 \\
+363 \\
\hline
\end{array}
\qquad
\begin{array}{r}
714 \\
+291 \\
\hline
\end{array}
\qquad
\begin{array}{r}
312 \\
+85 \\
\hline
\end{array}
$$

$$
\begin{array}{r}
300 \\
+547 \\
\hline
\end{array}
\qquad
\begin{array}{r}
591 \\
+120 \\
\hline
\end{array}
\qquad
\begin{array}{r}
612 \\
+319 \\
\hline
\end{array}
\qquad
\begin{array}{r}
425 \\
+125 \\
\hline
\end{array}
\qquad
\begin{array}{r}
411 \\
+120 \\
\hline
\end{array}
$$

$$
\begin{array}{r}
863 \\
+192 \\
\hline
\end{array}
\qquad
\begin{array}{r}
459 \\
+130 \\
\hline
\end{array}
\qquad
\begin{array}{r}
603 \\
+209 \\
\hline
\end{array}
\qquad
\begin{array}{r}
711 \\
+191 \\
\hline
\end{array}
\qquad
\begin{array}{r}
252 \\
+130 \\
\hline
\end{array}
$$

Lesson 5.11 Checking Subtraction with Addition

To check

$982 - 657 = 325$,

add 657 to 325.

$$\begin{array}{r} 982 \\ -657 \\ \hline 325 \\ +657 \\ \hline 982 \end{array}$$

These should be the same.

Subtract. Check each answer.

$$\begin{array}{r} 720 \\ -150 \\ \hline 570 \\ +150 \\ \hline 720 \end{array}$$

$$\begin{array}{r} 321 \\ -83 \\ \hline \end{array}$$

$$\begin{array}{r} 125 \\ -92 \\ \hline \end{array}$$

$$\begin{array}{r} 983 \\ -657 \\ \hline \end{array}$$

$$\begin{array}{r} 456 \\ -291 \\ \hline \end{array}$$

$$\begin{array}{r} 300 \\ -179 \\ \hline \end{array}$$

$$\begin{array}{r} 119 \\ -104 \\ \hline \end{array}$$

$$\begin{array}{r} 423 \\ -197 \\ \hline \end{array}$$

$$\begin{array}{r} 259 \\ -147 \\ \hline \end{array}$$

$$\begin{array}{r} 592 \\ -463 \\ \hline \end{array}$$

$$\begin{array}{r} 519 \\ -120 \\ \hline \end{array}$$

$$\begin{array}{r} 540 \\ -320 \\ \hline \end{array}$$

$$\begin{array}{r} 192 \\ -86 \\ \hline \end{array}$$

$$\begin{array}{r} 710 \\ -447 \\ \hline \end{array}$$

$$\begin{array}{r} 683 \\ -419 \\ \hline \end{array}$$

$$\begin{array}{r} 719 \\ -532 \\ \hline \end{array}$$

$$\begin{array}{r} 919 \\ -457 \\ \hline \end{array}$$

$$\begin{array}{r} 687 \\ -250 \\ \hline \end{array}$$

$$\begin{array}{r} 912 \\ -609 \\ \hline \end{array}$$

$$\begin{array}{r} 542 \\ -327 \\ \hline \end{array}$$

Lesson 5.12 Addition and Subtraction Practice

Add or subtract.

39 +92	86 +93	132 − 41	186 − 92	543 −121
76 +192	154 − 92	543 −206	150 − 90	650 +129
137 +310	159 − 82	185 − 96	432 −257	710 −512
541 +862	432 −119	720 +140	186 −107	540 − 75
812 + 93	712 −347	690 −320	451 −253	512 −308
119 +104	703 +219	861 −172	186 +210	513 −211

Lesson 5.12 Addition and Subtraction Practice

Add or subtract.

$$
\begin{array}{r} 120 \\ -45 \\ \hline \end{array}
\qquad
\begin{array}{r} 198 \\ -79 \\ \hline \end{array}
\qquad
\begin{array}{r} 312 \\ -192 \\ \hline \end{array}
\qquad
\begin{array}{r} 519 \\ +130 \\ \hline \end{array}
\qquad
\begin{array}{r} 710 \\ +195 \\ \hline \end{array}
$$

$$
\begin{array}{r} 412 \\ -306 \\ \hline \end{array}
\qquad
\begin{array}{r} 790 \\ -205 \\ \hline \end{array}
\qquad
\begin{array}{r} 157 \\ +192 \\ \hline \end{array}
\qquad
\begin{array}{r} 175 \\ -84 \\ \hline \end{array}
\qquad
\begin{array}{r} 192 \\ +210 \\ \hline \end{array}
$$

$$
\begin{array}{r} 510 \\ +834 \\ \hline \end{array}
\qquad
\begin{array}{r} 674 \\ -556 \\ \hline \end{array}
\qquad
\begin{array}{r} 700 \\ -310 \\ \hline \end{array}
\qquad
\begin{array}{r} 120 \\ +460 \\ \hline \end{array}
\qquad
\begin{array}{r} 690 \\ -541 \\ \hline \end{array}
$$

$$
\begin{array}{r} 898 \\ -844 \\ \hline \end{array}
\qquad
\begin{array}{r} 412 \\ -340 \\ \hline \end{array}
\qquad
\begin{array}{r} 775 \\ -436 \\ \hline \end{array}
\qquad
\begin{array}{r} 173 \\ +171 \\ \hline \end{array}
\qquad
\begin{array}{r} 100 \\ +761 \\ \hline \end{array}
$$

$$
\begin{array}{r} 962 \\ -841 \\ \hline \end{array}
\qquad
\begin{array}{r} 367 \\ +549 \\ \hline \end{array}
\qquad
\begin{array}{r} 829 \\ -394 \\ \hline \end{array}
\qquad
\begin{array}{r} 559 \\ +129 \\ \hline \end{array}
\qquad
\begin{array}{r} 796 \\ -318 \\ \hline \end{array}
$$

$$
\begin{array}{r} 710 \\ -696 \\ \hline \end{array}
\qquad
\begin{array}{r} 320 \\ +190 \\ \hline \end{array}
\qquad
\begin{array}{r} 971 \\ -320 \\ \hline \end{array}
\qquad
\begin{array}{r} 291 \\ +390 \\ \hline \end{array}
\qquad
\begin{array}{r} 220 \\ +557 \\ \hline \end{array}
$$

Lesson 5.12 Addition and Subtraction Practice

Add or subtract.

$$
\begin{array}{r} 72 \\ +59 \\ \hline \end{array}
\qquad
\begin{array}{r} 76 \\ +82 \\ \hline \end{array}
\qquad
\begin{array}{r} 138 \\ -\ 52 \\ \hline \end{array}
\qquad
\begin{array}{r} 192 \\ -\ 75 \\ \hline \end{array}
\qquad
\begin{array}{r} 310 \\ +354 \\ \hline \end{array}
$$

$$
\begin{array}{r} 191 \\ +210 \\ \hline \end{array}
\qquad
\begin{array}{r} 583 \\ -421 \\ \hline \end{array}
\qquad
\begin{array}{r} 710 \\ -190 \\ \hline \end{array}
\qquad
\begin{array}{r} 54 \\ +86 \\ \hline \end{array}
\qquad
\begin{array}{r} 93 \\ +104 \\ \hline \end{array}
$$

$$
\begin{array}{r} 582 \\ +529 \\ \hline \end{array}
\qquad
\begin{array}{r} 711 \\ -547 \\ \hline \end{array}
\qquad
\begin{array}{r} 712 \\ -\ 92 \\ \hline \end{array}
\qquad
\begin{array}{r} 860 \\ +139 \\ \hline \end{array}
\qquad
\begin{array}{r} 786 \\ -457 \\ \hline \end{array}
$$

$$
\begin{array}{r} 186 \\ +211 \\ \hline \end{array}
\qquad
\begin{array}{r} 210 \\ -102 \\ \hline \end{array}
\qquad
\begin{array}{r} 96 \\ +87 \\ \hline \end{array}
\qquad
\begin{array}{r} 310 \\ +\ 99 \\ \hline \end{array}
\qquad
\begin{array}{r} 386 \\ +503 \\ \hline \end{array}
$$

$$
\begin{array}{r} 232 \\ -144 \\ \hline \end{array}
\qquad
\begin{array}{r} 457 \\ -310 \\ \hline \end{array}
\qquad
\begin{array}{r} 386 \\ +205 \\ \hline \end{array}
\qquad
\begin{array}{r} 740 \\ -310 \\ \hline \end{array}
\qquad
\begin{array}{r} 862 \\ -456 \\ \hline \end{array}
$$

$$
\begin{array}{r} 392 \\ -\ 86 \\ \hline \end{array}
\qquad
\begin{array}{r} 510 \\ -\ 47 \\ \hline \end{array}
\qquad
\begin{array}{r} 610 \\ -232 \\ \hline \end{array}
\qquad
\begin{array}{r} 192 \\ -\ 86 \\ \hline \end{array}
\qquad
\begin{array}{r} 191 \\ +212 \\ \hline \end{array}
$$

Check What You Learned

SHOW YOUR WORK

Working with 3-Digit Numbers

Count by 5.

100, 105, _____, _____, 120, _____, _____, 135

Count by 10.

650, _____, 670, _____, _____, 700, _____, 720

Count by 100.

375, _____, 575, _____, _____, _____, 975

Write the number and its expanded form or number name.

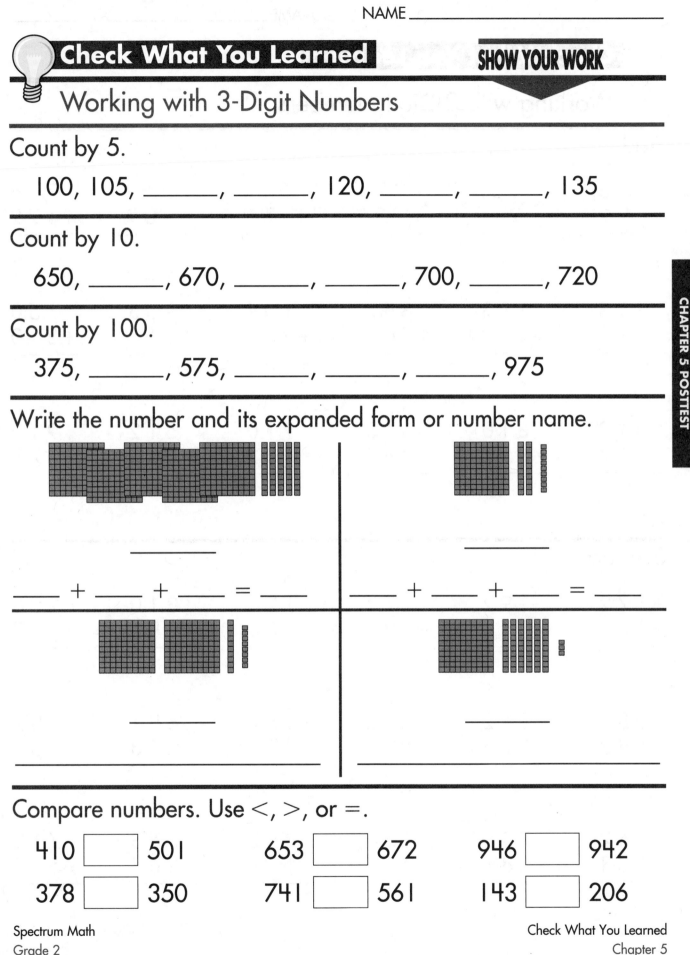

_____

___ + ___ + ___ = ___

_____

___ + ___ + ___ = ___

_____

_____

Compare numbers. Use <, >, or =.

410 ☐ 501   653 ☐ 672   946 ☐ 942

378 ☐ 350   741 ☐ 561   143 ☐ 206

Check What You Learned

Working with 3-Digit Numbers

Add.

75 +92	135 +210	193 + 56	310 + 92	513 +409	746 +122
193 + 86	183 +192	842 +908	109 +236	963 +310	150 +210
512 +457	310 + 97	510 +346	910 +132	512 +403	912 + 78

Subtract.

172 - 35	192 - 86	174 - 96	120 - 80	310 - 40	293 -107
986 -698	862 -245	352 -121	187 - 72	647 -253	547 -183
662 -503	708 -231	456 -269	882 -199	753 -268	712 -543

Check What You Know

Measurement

Estimate the length of each object. Then, use a ruler to measure each object in inches and centimeters.

Estimate: _____ in. _____ cm   Estimate: _____ in. _____ cm

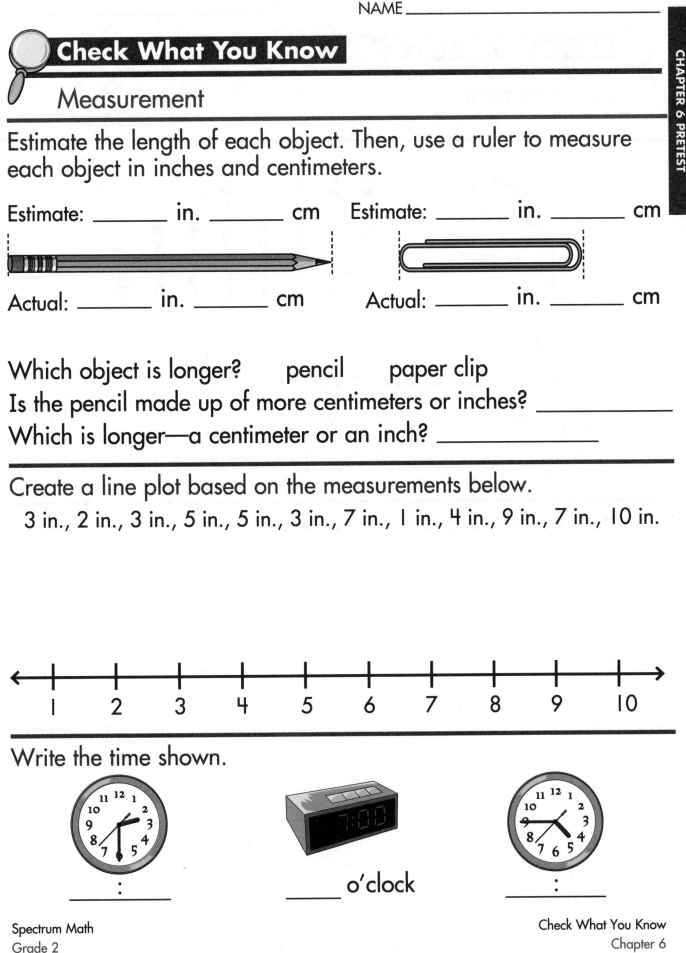

Actual: _____ in. _____ cm   Actual: _____ in. _____ cm

Which object is longer?   pencil   paper clip

Is the pencil made up of more centimeters or inches? _____

Which is longer—a centimeter or an inch? _____

Create a line plot based on the measurements below.

3 in., 2 in., 3 in., 5 in., 5 in., 3 in., 7 in., 1 in., 4 in., 9 in., 7 in., 10 in.

Write the time shown.

_____ : _____   _____ o'clock   _____ : _____

NAME _____

Check What You Know

Measurement

Favorite Ice Cream Flavors

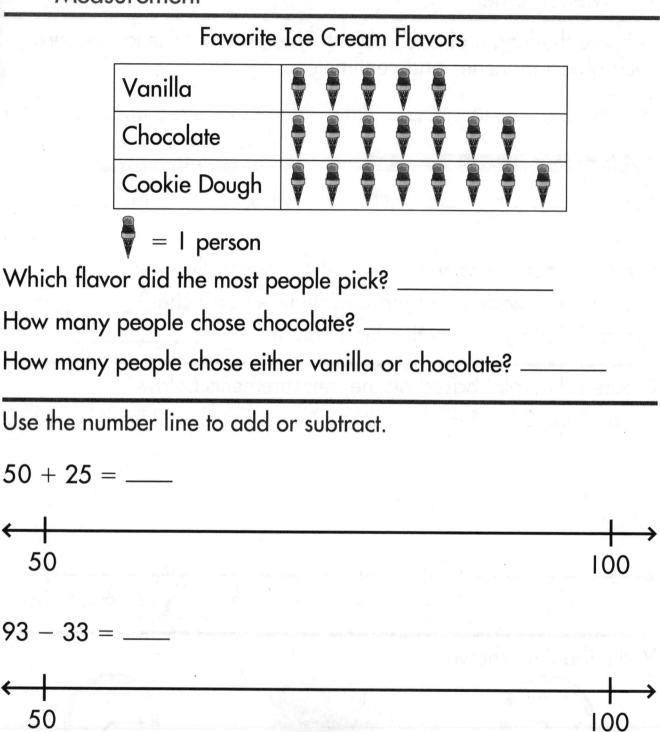

= 1 person

Which flavor did the most people pick? _____

How many people chose chocolate? _____

How many people chose either vanilla or chocolate? _____

Use the number line to add or subtract.

$50 + 25 =$ _____

```
←——+————————————————————+——→
   50                    100
```

$93 - 33 =$ _____

```
←——+————————————————————+——→
   50                    100
```

Lesson 6.2 Telling Time to the Half Hour

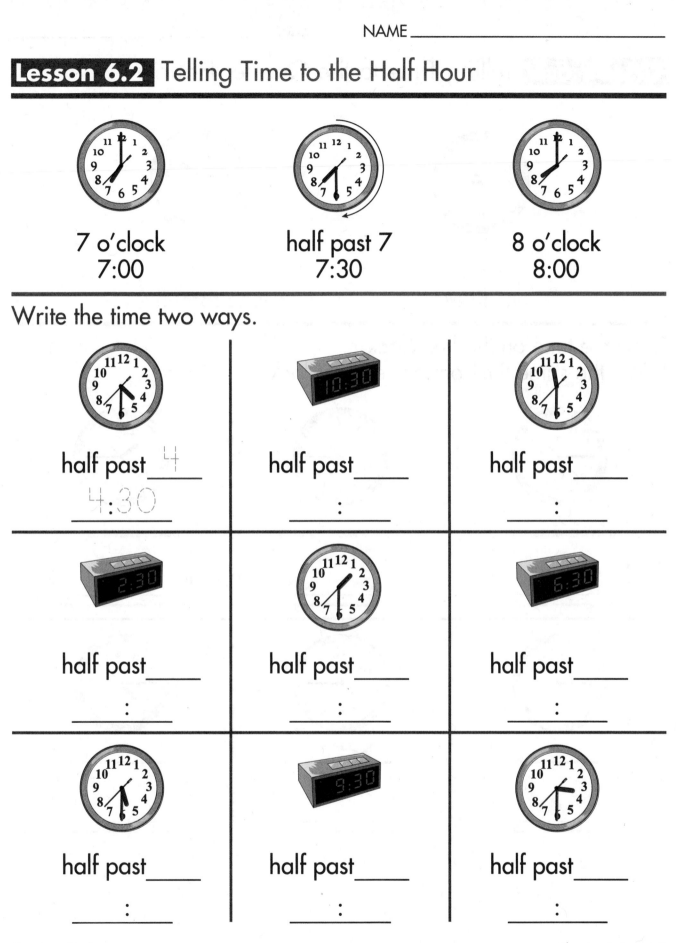

7 o'clock
7:00

half past 7
7:30

8 o'clock
8:00

Write the time two ways.

half past ___4___

___4:30___

half past _____

_____:_____

half past _____

_____:_____

half past _____

_____:_____

half past _____

_____:_____

half past _____

_____:_____

half past _____

_____:_____

half past _____

_____:_____

half past _____

_____:_____

Lesson 6.3 Telling Time to the Quarter Hour

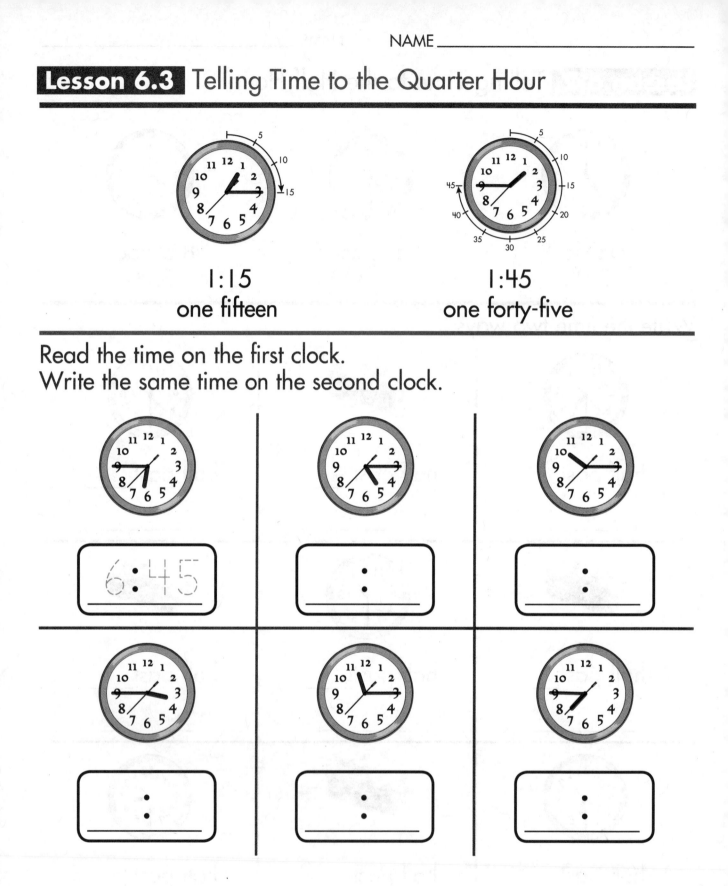

1:15
one fifteen

1:45
one forty-five

Read the time on the first clock.
Write the same time on the second clock.

6:45

:

:

:

:

:

Lesson 6.3 Problem Solving

Solve each problem.

The small hand is between __3__ and __4__.

The large hand is on the __6__.

The time is __3:30__.

The small hand is between _____ and _____.

The large hand is on the _____.

The time is ____:____.

The small hand is on the _____.

The large hand is on the _____.

The time is ____:____.

The small hand is between _____ and _____.

The large hand is on the _____.

The time is ____:____.

The small hand is on the _____.

The large hand is on the _____.

The time is ____:____.

NAME _____

Lesson 6.4 Estimating Inches

Estimate how many inches long each object is.

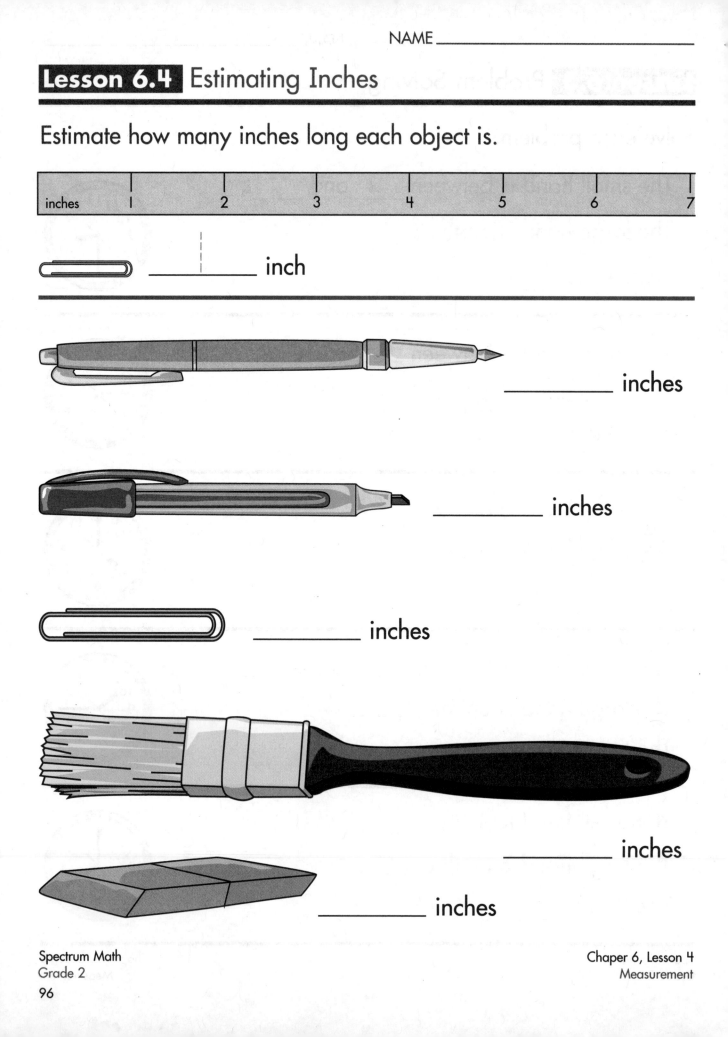

_____ inch

_____ inches

_____ inches

_____ inches

_____ inches

_____ inches

Lesson 6.5 Estimating Centimeters

Estimate how many centimeters long each object is.

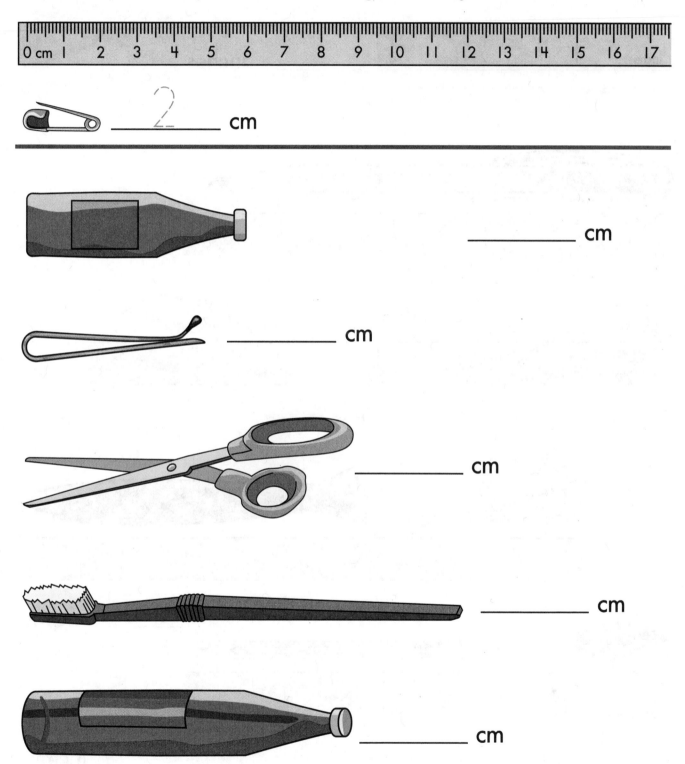

2 _____ cm

_____ cm

_____ cm

_____ cm

_____ cm

_____ cm

Lesson 6.6 Measuring Length in Inches

Write the length of each object in inches.

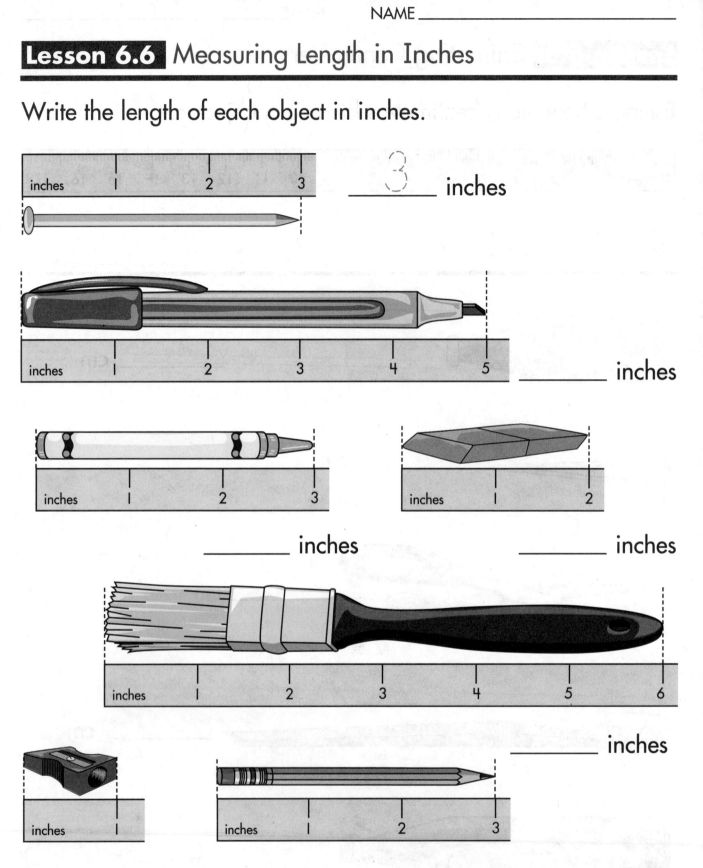

_____ inches

_____ inches

_____ inches

_____ inches

_____ inches

_____ inch

_____ inches

Lesson 6.7 Making a Line Plot

Answer the questions below using the previous page.

How many objects measured 1 inch? _____

How many objects measured 2 inches? _____

How many objects measured 3 inches? _____

How many objects measured 4 inches? _____

How many objects measured 5 inches? _____

How many objects measured 6 inches? _____

Make a line plot using the information above.

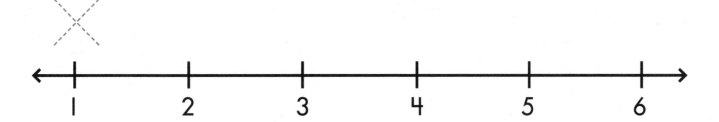

Lesson 6.8 Measuring Length in Inches

Perimeter is the length
around an object.

The perimeter of this hexagon is

1 + 1 + 1 + 1 + 1 + 1 = 6 inches.

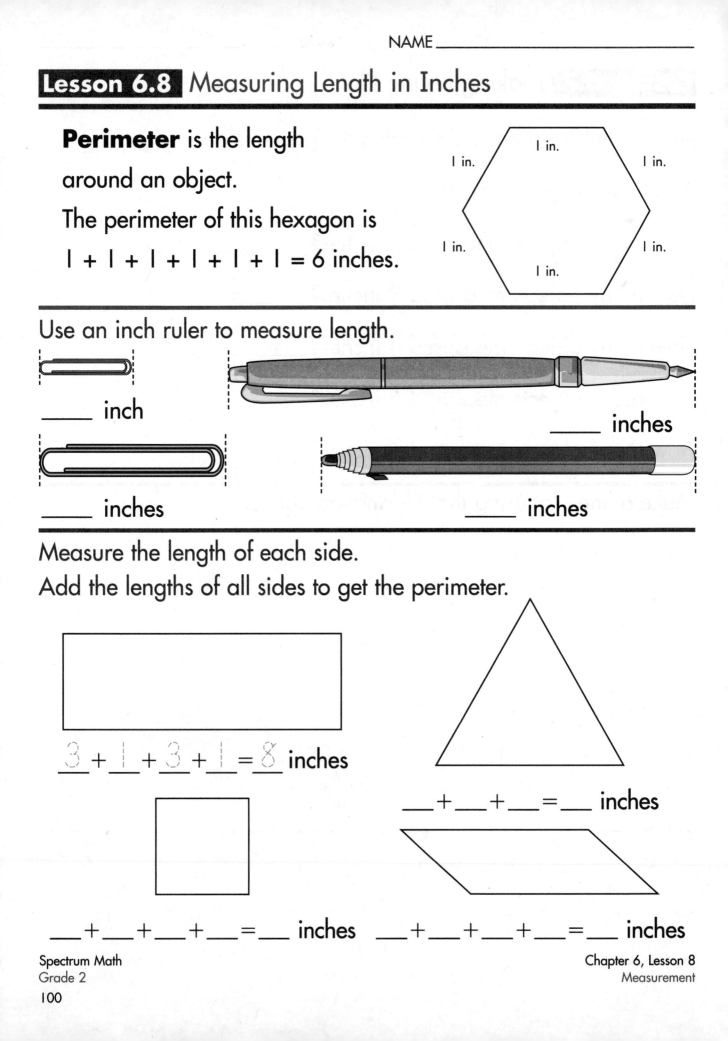

1 in.

1 in.   1 in.

1 in.   1 in.

1 in.

Use an inch ruler to measure length.

_____ inch

_____ inches

_____ inches

_____ inches

Measure the length of each side.
Add the lengths of all sides to get the perimeter.

_3_ + _1_ + _3_ + _1_ = _8_ inches

__ + __ + __ = __ inches

__ + __ + __ + __ = __ inches

__ + __ + __ + __ = __ inches

Lesson 6.9 Making a Line Plot

Create a line plot using the length of each shape.

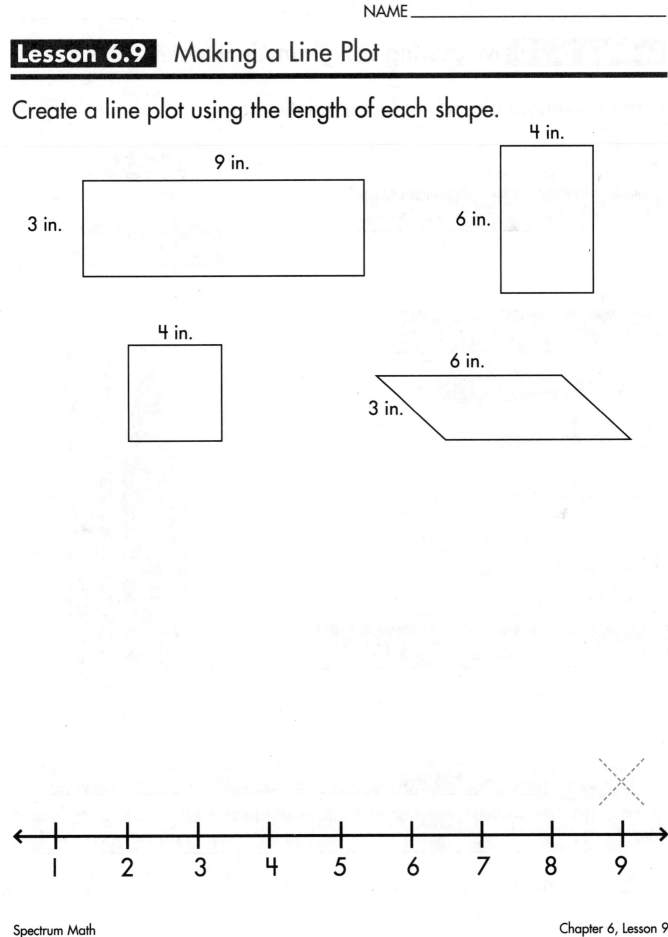

Lesson 6.10 Measuring Length in Centimeters

Write the length of each object in centimeters.

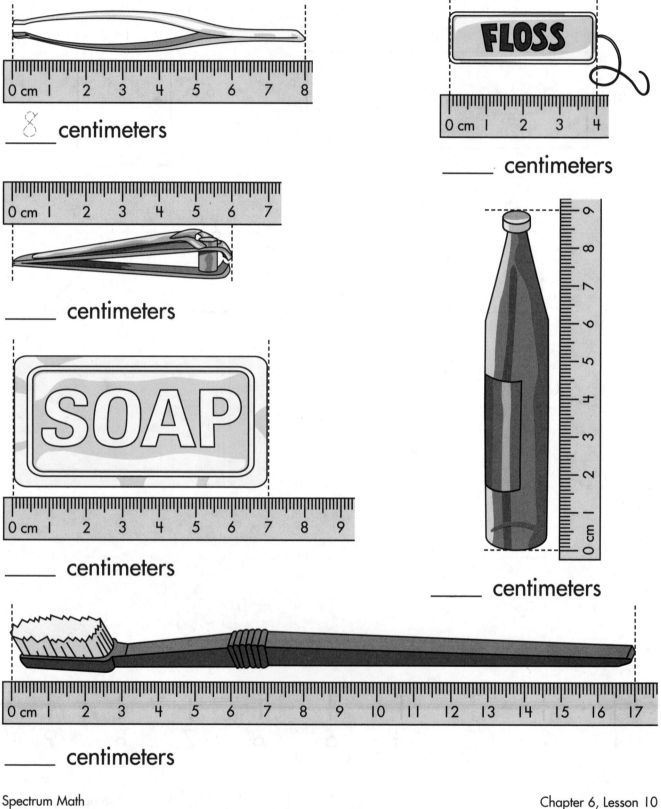

_____ centimeters

_____ centimeters

_____ centimeters

_____ centimeters

_____ centimeters

_____ centimeters

Lesson 6.11 Making a Line Plot

Create a line plot based on the measurements below.

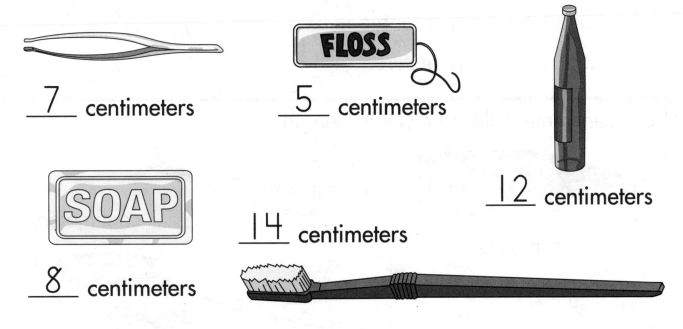

__7__ centimeters

__5__ centimeters

__12__ centimeters

__8__ centimeters

__14__ centimeters

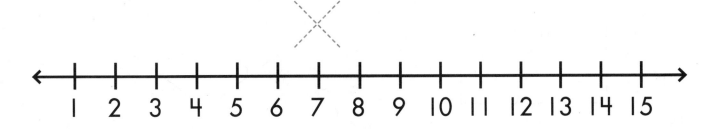

<←——┼——┼——┼——┼——┼——┼——┼——┼——┼——┼——┼——┼——┼——┼——┼——→
1 2 3 4 5 6 7 8 9 10 11 12 13 14 15

Lesson 6.12 Measuring Length in Centimeters

You can measure perimeter in centimeters.

The perimeter of this triangle is

$3 + 3 + 3 = 9$ centimeters.

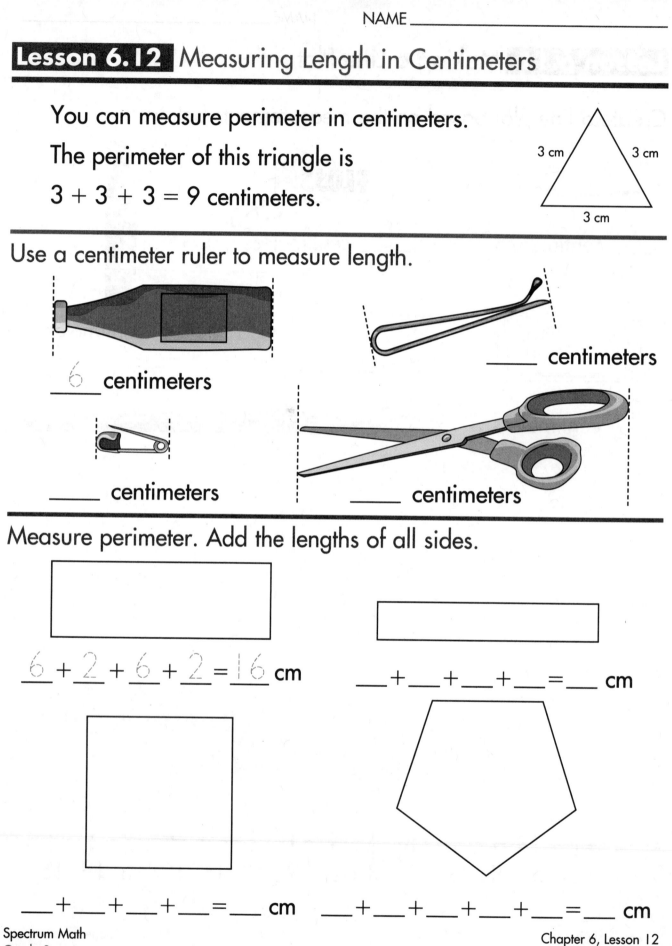

Use a centimeter ruler to measure length.

_6_ centimeters

_____ centimeters

_____ centimeters

_____ centimeters

Measure perimeter. Add the lengths of all sides.

_6_ + _2_ + _6_ + _2_ = _16_ cm

___ + ___ + ___ + ___ = ___ cm

___ + ___ + ___ + ___ = ___ cm

___ + ___ + ___ + ___ + ___ = ___ cm

Lesson 6.13 Making a Line Plot

Create a line plot using the length of each shape.

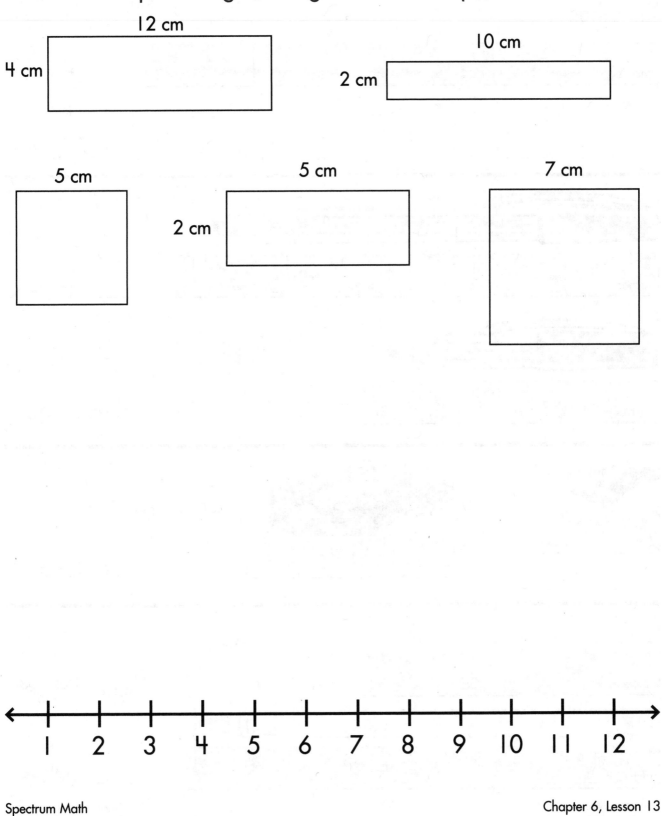

Lesson 6.14 How Much Longer?

Measure each object. Tell how much longer one object is than the other.

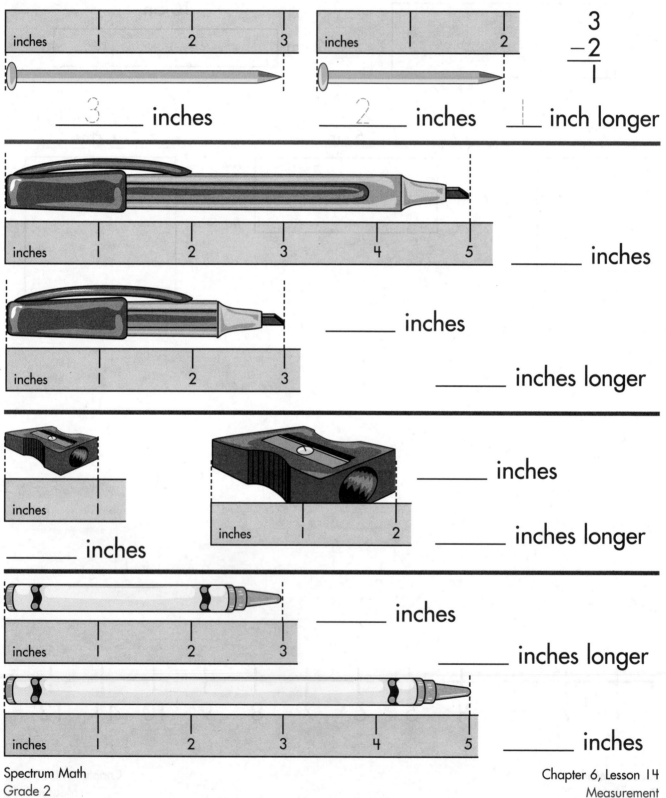

$$\begin{array}{r} 3 \\ -2 \\ \hline 1 \end{array}$$

_____3_____ inches   _____2_____ inches   __1__ inch longer

_____ inches

_____ inches

_____ inches longer

_____ inches

_____ inches

_____ inches longer

_____ inches

_____ inches longer

_____ inches

Lesson 6.15 How Much Longer?

Measure each object. Tell how much longer one object is than the other.

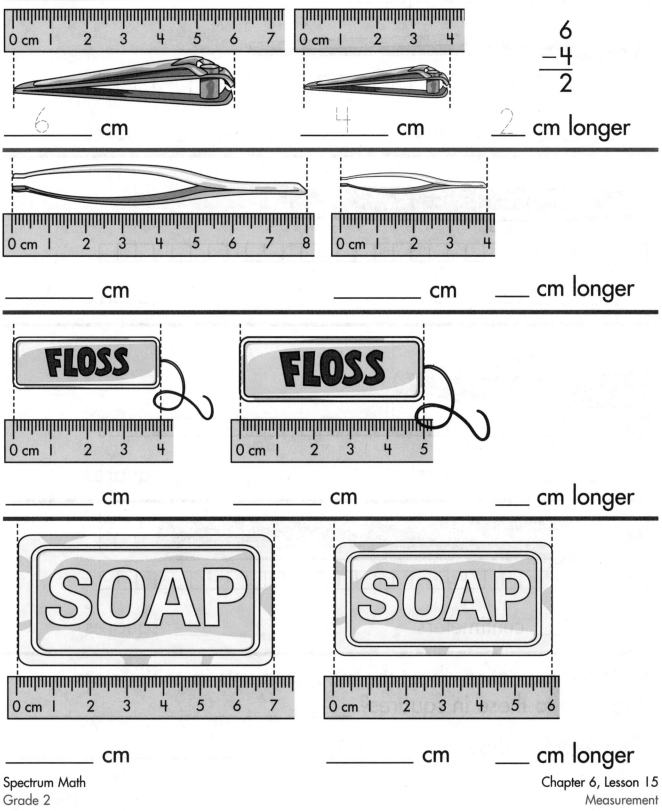

$$\begin{array}{r} 6 \\ -4 \\ \hline 2 \end{array}$$

_6_ cm   _4_ cm   _2_ cm longer

_____ cm   _____ cm   ___ cm longer

_____ cm   _____ cm   ___ cm longer

_____ cm   _____ cm   ___ cm longer

NAME_____

Lesson 6.16 Comparing Measurements

Use a ruler to measure each object in centimeters. Then, measure again using the line of squares.

_____11_____ centimeters   _____22_____ squares

_____ centimeters   _____ squares

_____ centimeters   _____ squares

_____ centimeters   _____ squares

What do you notice about the measurements in centimeters compared to those in squares? _____

What explains this? _____

Spectrum Math
Grade 2
108

Chapter 6, Lesson 16
Measurement

Lesson 6.16 Comparing Measurements

Use a ruler to measure each object in centimeters. Then, measure again to the nearest inch.

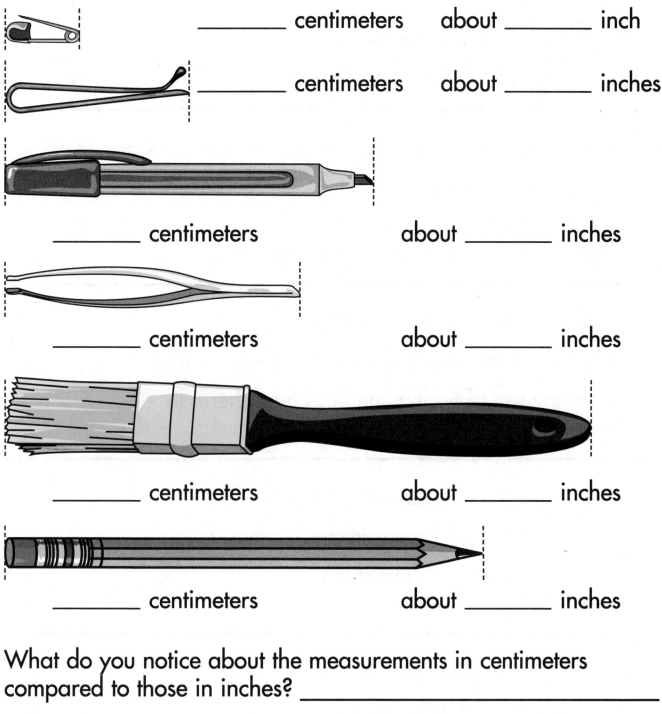

_____ centimeters   about _____ inch

_____ centimeters   about _____ inches

_____ centimeters   about _____ inches

_____ centimeters   about _____ inches

_____ centimeters   about _____ inches

_____ centimeters   about _____ inches

What do you notice about the measurements in centimeters compared to those in inches? _____

What explains this? _____

Lesson 6.17 Problem Solving

Solve each problem.

Ryan has 48 feet of ribbon.

$$\begin{array}{r} 48 \\ + 21 \\ \hline 69 \end{array}$$

Sierra has 21 feet of ribbon.

How many feet of ribbon do they have altogether? ____69____

Miranda has 11 inches of border for the bulletin board.

She needs 27 inches.

How much more border does
Miranda need to finish the bulletin board? _____

A fisherman had 20 feet of fishing line.

His line got stuck, and he had to cut away 13 feet.

How many feet of fishing line does the fisherman
have left? _____

Lindsey's necklace measured 17 inches.

Dominique's necklace measured 25 inches.

How much longer is Dominique's
necklace than Lindsey's? _____

Alfonzo's belt is 55 inches long.

Joshua's belt is 70 inches long.

How much longer is Joshua's belt than Alfonzo's? _____

Lesson 6.18 Reading Picture and Bar Graphs

Keisha asked her classmates about their pets.

She made this bar graph to show the results.

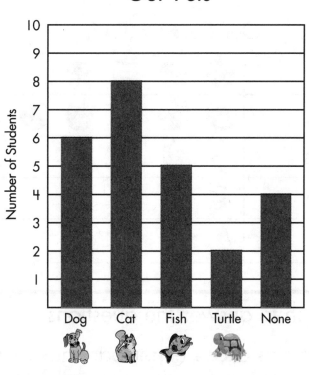

Our Pets

Use the bar graph to answer the questions.

How many students have a dog or a cat? __14__

How many students have no pets? _____

Which pet do the most students have? _____

How many students have either a fish or turtle? _____

How many students did Keisha talk to? _____

Lesson 6.18 Reading Picture and Bar Graphs

Carlos polled his classmates about their favorite fruits.
He made this picture graph with the results. One piece of fruit
on the graph means one person.

Our Favorite Fruits

Apples	🍎 🍎 🍎 🍎
Oranges	🍊 🍊 🍊 🍊 🍊 🍊
Bananas	🍌 🍌 🍌 🍌
Grapes	🍇 🍇 🍇
Pears	🍐 🍐 🍐 🍐

Use the picture graph to answer the questions.

How many classmates chose either bananas or oranges? __10__

How many chose grapes or pears? _____

Which fruit did the most classmates choose? _____

How many classmates did not choose oranges? _____

How many more chose apples than chose grapes? _____

How many classmates told Carlos their favorite fruit? _____

Lesson 6.18 Reading Picture and Bar Graphs

Sam and his friends collect baseball cards. This picture graph shows how many cards they have.

Our Baseball Cards

Sam	🂠 🂠 🂠 🂠 🂠 🂠
Tara	🂠 🂠 🂠 🂠 🂠
Kono	🂠 🂠 🂠 🂠 🂠 🂠
Trina	🂠 🂠 🂠 🂠

🂠 = 2 baseball cards

Use the picture graph to answer the questions.

How many cards do the friends have in all? ___40___

How many cards does Sam have? _____

Who has the fewest cards? _____

How many cards does Kono have? _____

How many cards do Tara and Trina have together? _____

How many more cards do
Tara and Trina have together compared to Sam? _____

Lesson 6.19 Creating a Bar Graph

Use the information in the tally chart to complete the bar graph.

Points in the Basketball Game

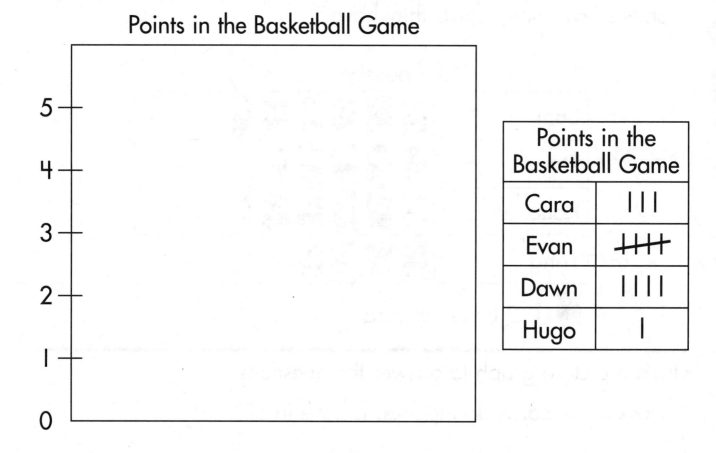

Points in the Basketball Game	
Cara	III
Evan	⧄IIII
Dawn	IIII
Hugo	I

Use the bar graph to answer the questions.

Which student scored the most points? _____

Which student scored the least points? _____

How many points were scored
altogether in the basketball game? _____

How many more points did Evan score than Hugo? _____

Lesson 6.20 Creating a Picture Graph

Use the information in the tally chart to complete the picture graph.

Shapes Around the Room	
Triangles	
Stars	
Squares	
Circles	

Shapes Around the Room	
▲	‖‖‖ ‖
☆	‖‖‖ ‖‖‖
■	‖‖‖ ‖‖‖‖
⬤	‖‖‖ ‖

Use the picture graph to answer the questions below.

What shape is seen the most around the room? _____

What shape is seen the least around the room? _____

How many more stars ☆ are there than triangles ▲ ? _____

How many more squares ■ are there than circles ⬤ ? _____

Lesson 6.21 Adding and Subtracting on a Number Line

Use the number line to add.

$$\begin{array}{r} 1\,0 \\ +3\,0 \\ \hline 4\,0 \end{array}$$

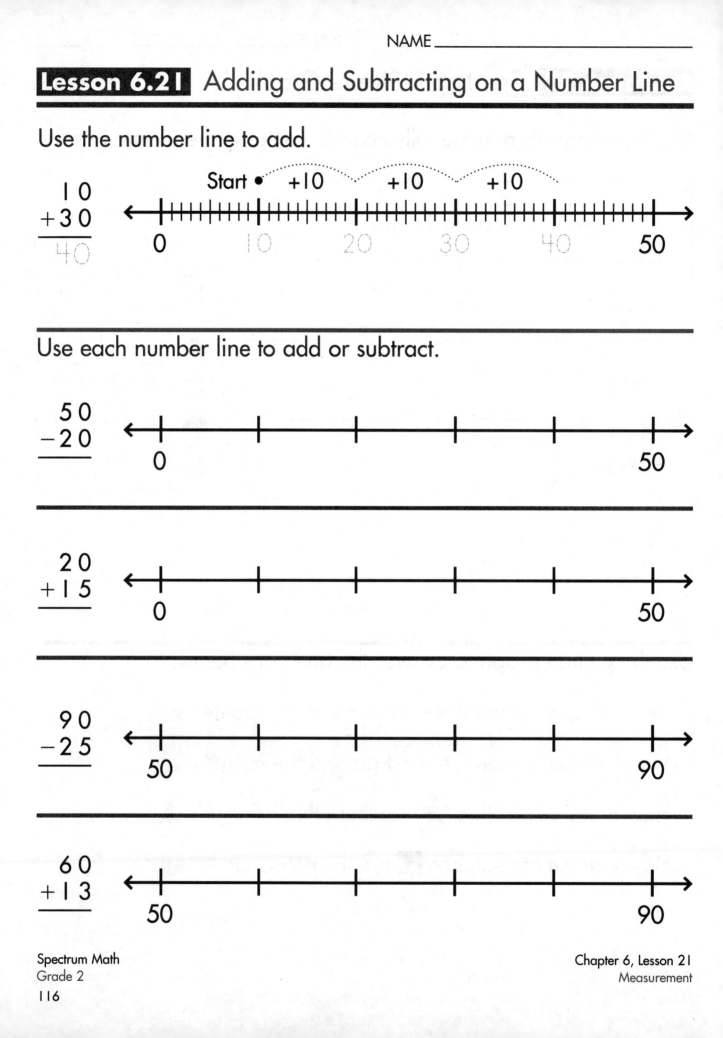

Use each number line to add or subtract.

$$\begin{array}{r} 5\,0 \\ -2\,0 \\ \hline \end{array}$$

$$\begin{array}{r} 2\,0 \\ +1\,5 \\ \hline \end{array}$$

$$\begin{array}{r} 9\,0 \\ -2\,5 \\ \hline \end{array}$$

$$\begin{array}{r} 6\,0 \\ +1\,3 \\ \hline \end{array}$$

Lesson 6.22 Problem Solving

Solve each problem.

$\begin{array}{r} 10 \\ 10 \end{array}$

Logan had 2 dimes.

He found 4 pennies in the couch cushions.

How much money does Logan have now? ___24¢___

$\begin{array}{r} +1 \\ \hline 24 \end{array}$

Amber has 1 nickel.

Justin has 7 pennies.

How much money do they have altogether? _____

Bonnie has 1 dime and 6 pennies.

How much money does she have? _____

Ben pulls 2 one-dollar bills, 1 quarter, 1 dime, 4 nickels, and 10 pennies from his piggy bank.

How much money does Ben have? _____

Casey's mother put a one-dollar bill, 2 quarters, 4 dimes, 1 nickel, and 5 pennies in an envelope for Casey to use at the book fair.

How much money did Casey's mother give Casey for the book fair? _____

Check What You Learned

Measurement

Estimate the length of each object. Then, use a ruler to measure each object in inches and centimeters.

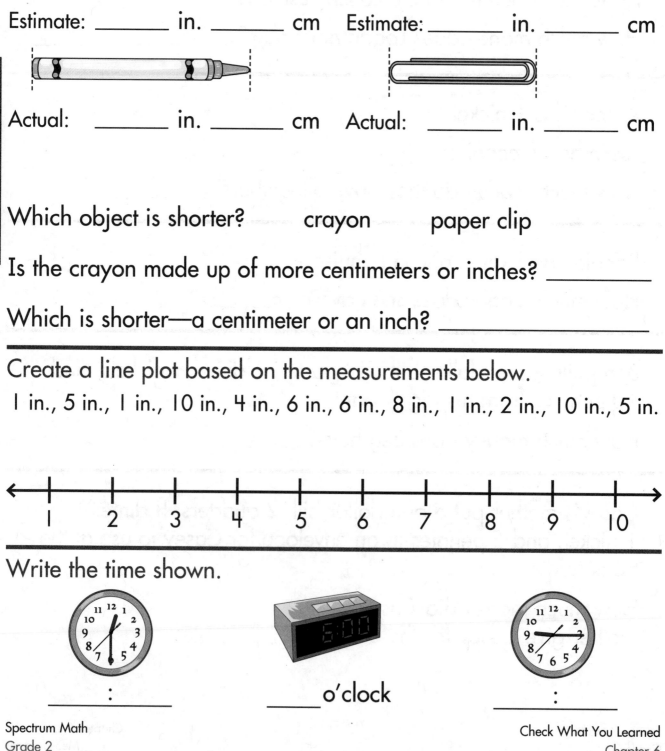

Estimate: _____ in. _____ cm   Estimate: _____ in. _____ cm

Actual: _____ in. _____ cm   Actual: _____ in. _____ cm

Which object is shorter?   crayon   paper clip

Is the crayon made up of more centimeters or inches? _____

Which is shorter—a centimeter or an inch? _____

Create a line plot based on the measurements below.

1 in., 5 in., 1 in., 10 in., 4 in., 6 in., 6 in., 8 in., 1 in., 2 in., 10 in., 5 in.

Write the time shown.

_____ : _____   _____ o'clock   _____ : _____

CHAPTER 6 POSTTEST

Check What You Learned

Measurement

Favorite Sports

Baseball	🥎 🥎 🥎 🥎 🥎 🥎 🥎
Football	🏈 🏈 🏈 🏈 🏈
Basketball	🏀 🏀 🏀 🏀 🏀 🏀
Soccer	⚽ ⚽ ⚽ ⚽ ⚽ ⚽ ⚽ ⚽

Use the picture graph to answer the questions. Each picture equals one person.

Which sport did most people choose? _____

Which sport did 7 people choose? _____

How many people chose football or basketball? _____

Use the number line to add or subtract.

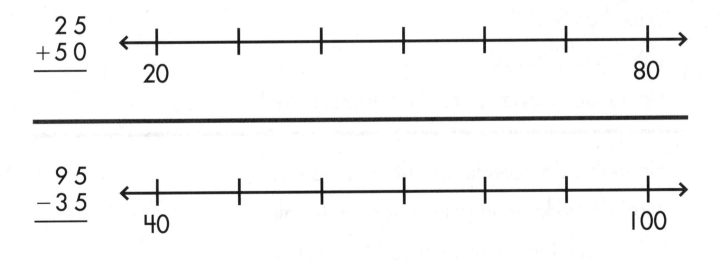

$$\begin{array}{r} 2\,5 \\ +5\,0 \\ \hline \end{array}$$

$$\begin{array}{r} 9\,5 \\ -3\,5 \\ \hline \end{array}$$

Check What You Learned

Measurement

Solve each problem.

Jordan was selling frozen treats.

Blake gave Jordan 2 quarters and 2 nickels.

How much did Blake pay for the treat? _____

Matthew's dad is 70 inches tall.

Orlando's dad is 78 inches tall.

How much taller is Orlando's dad than Matthew's? _____

Megan has $4.00.

She earns $2.50 more.

How much money does Megan have now? _____

Erica has $0.55.

Later, she finds $0.25.

How much money does Erica have now? _____

Hannah's dog can jump 8 feet in the air.

Maricela's dog can jump 6 feet in the air.

How much higher can Hannah's dog jump
than Maricela's? _____.

Check What You Learned

Geometry

Name each shape.

_____   _____   _____   _____

_____   _____   _____   _____

Circle the shape named.

square pyramid

cube

sphere

Answer the questions.

Which shape has 6 equal faces? _____

Which shape has 2 pairs of equal sides? _____

Which shape has 5 total angles? _____

Which shape is completely round and 3-D? _____

Check What You Learned

Geometry

Draw the plane shapes. Color them.

pentagon   rectangle

Draw the solid shapes. Color them.

square pyramid   cube

Circle the plane shapes that are faces on the solid shape.

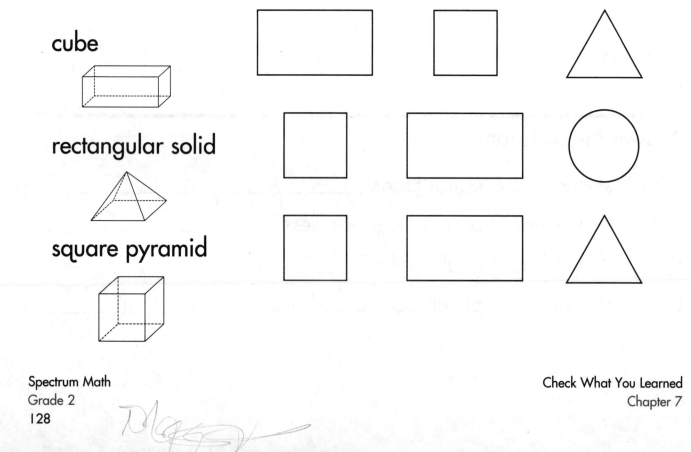

cube

rectangular solid

square pyramid

Check What You Know

Parts of a Whole

Complete.

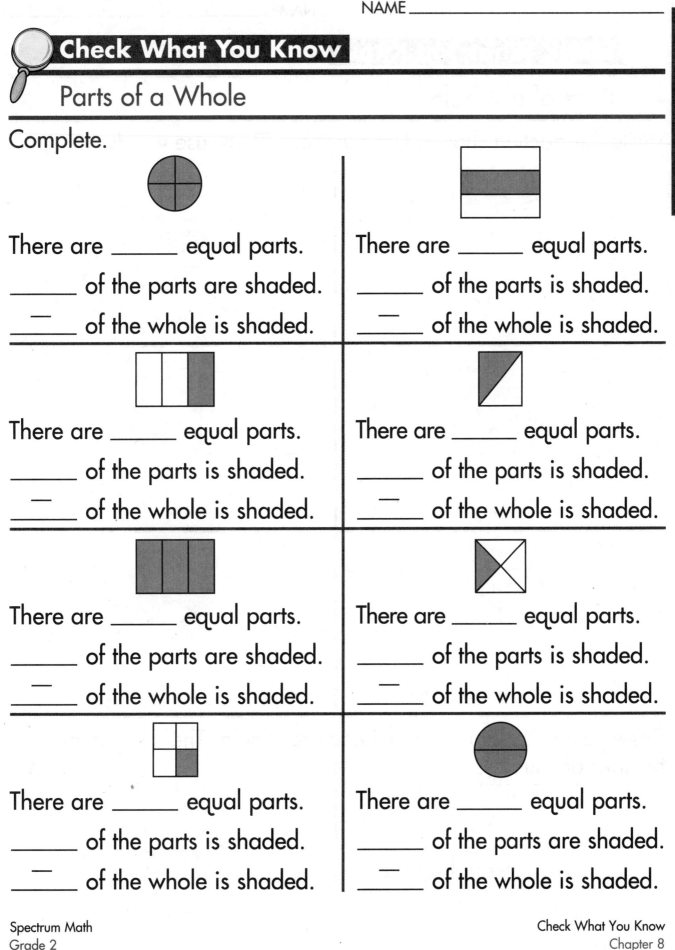

There are _____ equal parts.

_____ of the parts are shaded.

_____ of the whole is shaded.

There are _____ equal parts.

_____ of the parts is shaded.

_____ of the whole is shaded.

There are _____ equal parts.

_____ of the parts is shaded.

_____ of the whole is shaded.

There are _____ equal parts.

_____ of the parts is shaded.

_____ of the whole is shaded.

There are _____ equal parts.

_____ of the parts are shaded.

_____ of the whole is shaded.

There are _____ equal parts.

_____ of the parts is shaded.

_____ of the whole is shaded.

There are _____ equal parts.

_____ of the parts is shaded.

_____ of the whole is shaded.

There are _____ equal parts.

_____ of the parts are shaded.

_____ of the whole is shaded.

NAME _____

Check What You Know

Parts of a Whole

Write the fraction shown. Use numbers. Then, use words.

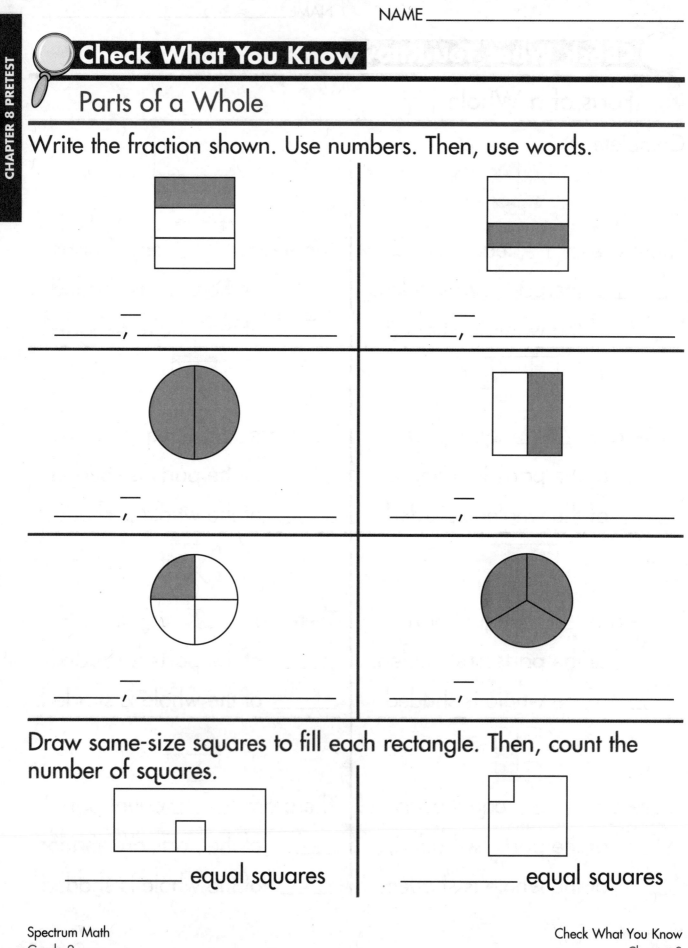

——— , ———————————

$\dfrac{\quad}{\quad}$, ———————————

——— , ———————————

$\dfrac{\quad}{\quad}$, ———————————

——— , ———————————

$\dfrac{\quad}{\quad}$, ———————————

Draw same-size squares to fill each rectangle. Then, count the number of squares.

_____ equal squares

_____ equal squares

Lesson 8.1 Parts of Shapes

A shape can be broken into equal parts. These equal parts are called **fractions**.

A **half** is one of two equal parts. 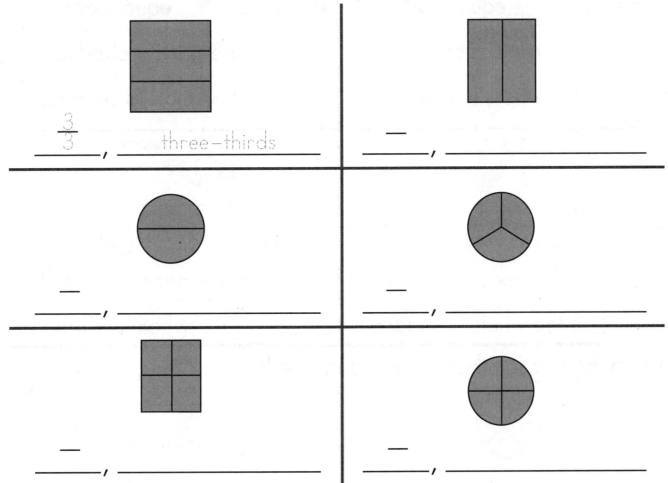 Two halves make a whole. ⬕.
The fraction **two-halves** means 2 out of 2 total parts, or $\frac{2}{2}$.

A **third** is one of three equal parts. ⬕ Three thirds make a whole. ⬕
The fraction **three-thirds** means 3 out of 3 total parts, or $\frac{3}{3}$.

A **fourth** is one of four equal parts. ⬕ Four fourths make a whole. ⬕

The fraction **four-fourths** means 4 out of 4 total parts, or $\frac{4}{4}$.

Write the fraction shown. Use numbers. Then, use words.

$\frac{3}{3}$, three-thirds

___ , ___

___ , ___

___ , ___

___ , ___

___ , ___

Lesson 8.2 One-Half

One-half of the whole is shaded.

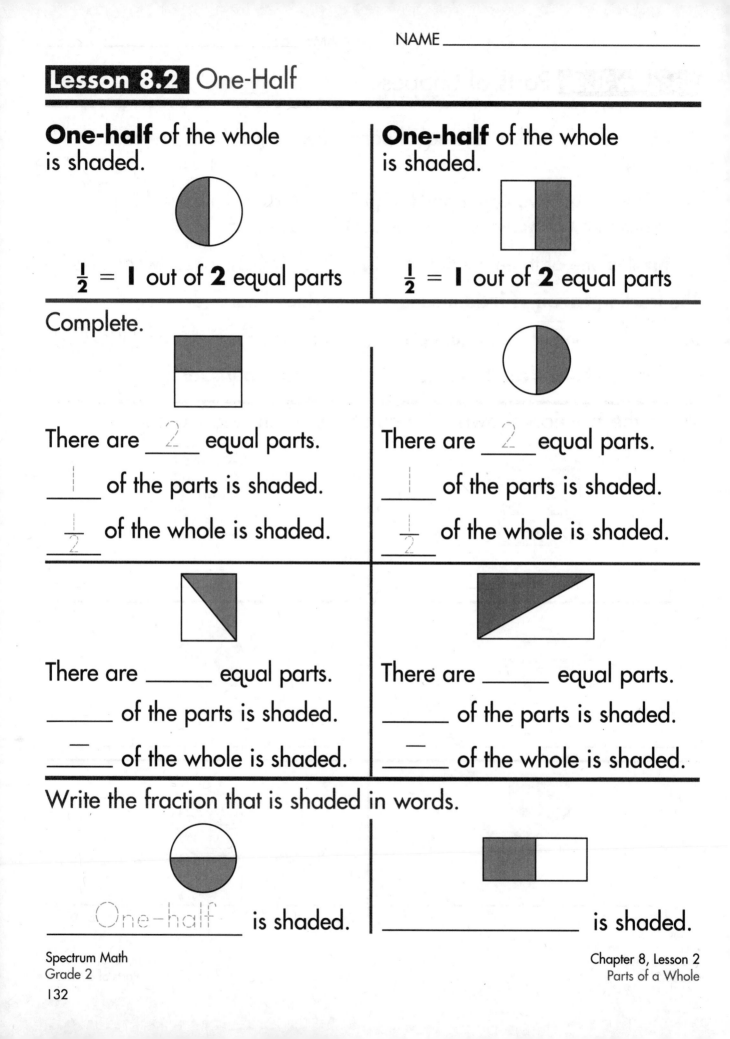

$\frac{1}{2}$ = **1** out of **2** equal parts

One-half of the whole is shaded.

$\frac{1}{2}$ = **1** out of **2** equal parts

Complete.

There are __2__ equal parts.

__1__ of the parts is shaded.

$\frac{1}{2}$ of the whole is shaded.

There are __2__ equal parts.

__1__ of the parts is shaded.

$\frac{1}{2}$ of the whole is shaded.

There are _____ equal parts.

_____ of the parts is shaded.

$\frac{}{}$ of the whole is shaded.

There are _____ equal parts.

_____ of the parts is shaded.

$\frac{}{}$ of the whole is shaded.

Write the fraction that is shaded in words.

One-half is shaded.

_____ is shaded.

Lesson 8.3 One-Third

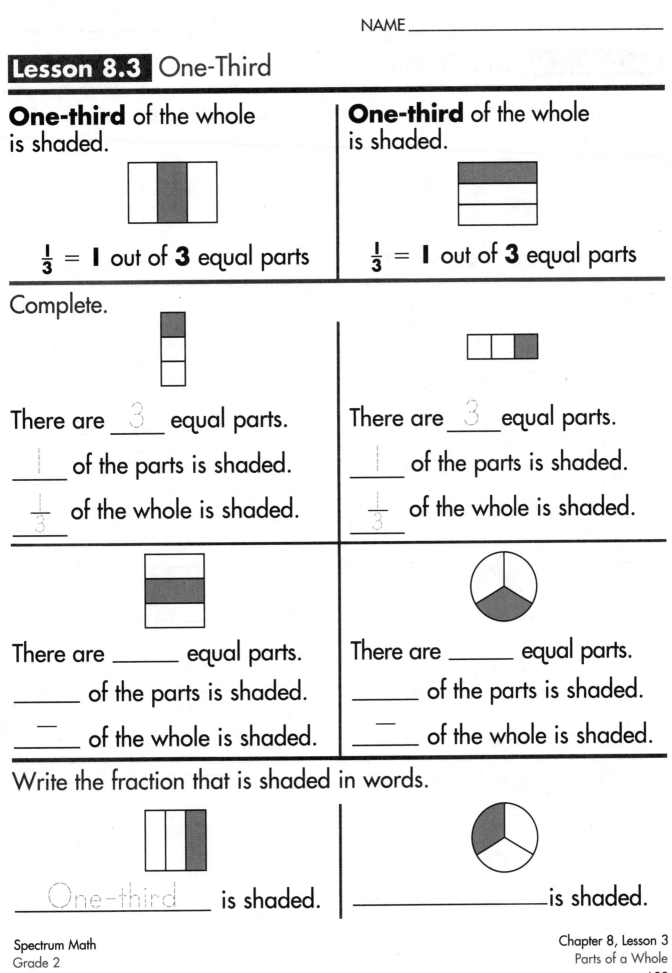

One-third of the whole is shaded.

$\frac{1}{3}$ = **1** out of **3** equal parts

One-third of the whole is shaded.

$\frac{1}{3}$ = **1** out of **3** equal parts

Complete.

There are ___3___ equal parts.

___1___ of the parts is shaded.

___1___ of the whole is shaded.
$\overline{3}$

There are ___3___ equal parts.

___1___ of the parts is shaded.

___1___ of the whole is shaded.
$\overline{3}$

There are _____ equal parts.

_____ of the parts is shaded.

_____ of the whole is shaded.

There are _____ equal parts.

_____ of the parts is shaded.

_____ of the whole is shaded.

Write the fraction that is shaded in words.

___One-third___ is shaded.

_____ is shaded.

Lesson 8.4 One-Fourth

One-fourth of the whole is shaded.

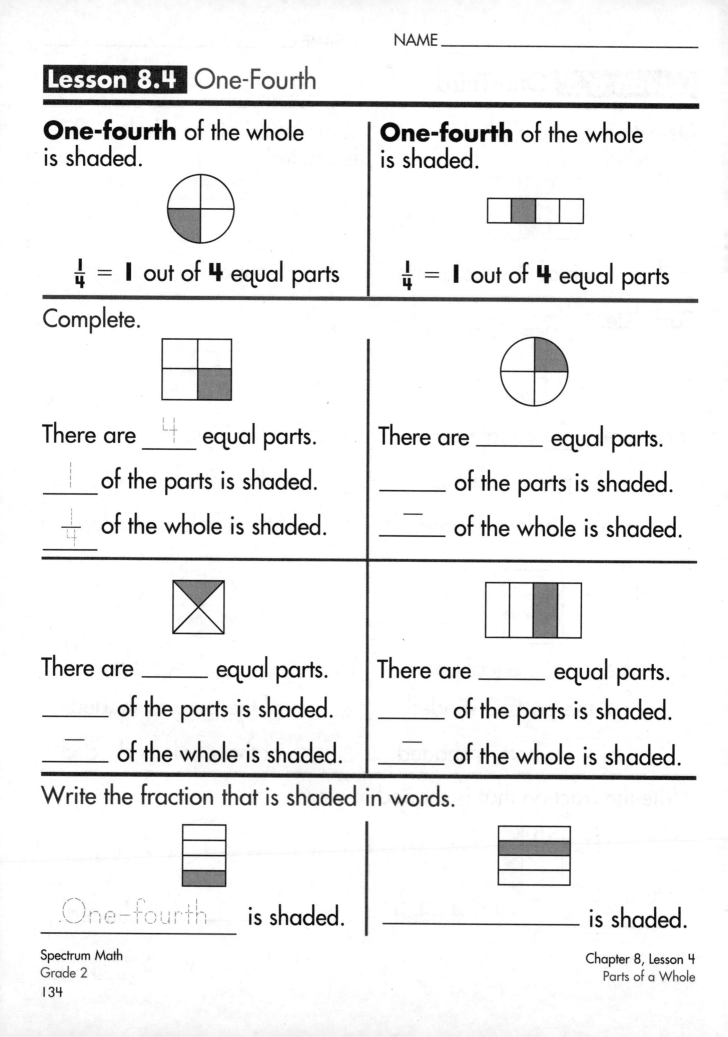

$\frac{1}{4}$ = **1** out of **4** equal parts

One-fourth of the whole is shaded.

$\frac{1}{4}$ = **1** out of **4** equal parts

Complete.

There are __4__ equal parts.

__1__ of the parts is shaded.

$\frac{1}{4}$ of the whole is shaded.

There are _____ equal parts.

_____ of the parts is shaded.

$\frac{\quad}{\quad}$ of the whole is shaded.

There are _____ equal parts.

_____ of the parts is shaded.

$\frac{\quad}{\quad}$ of the whole is shaded.

There are _____ equal parts.

_____ of the parts is shaded.

$\frac{\quad}{\quad}$ of the whole is shaded.

Write the fraction that is shaded in words.

One-fourth _____ is shaded.

_____ is shaded.

Lesson 8.5 Partitioning Rectangles

Rectangles can be divided up into same-size squares to show how much space they cover.

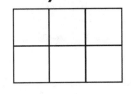

This rectangle is made up of 6 squares. It takes up 6 squares of space.

Count the squares ▢ that make up each rectangle.

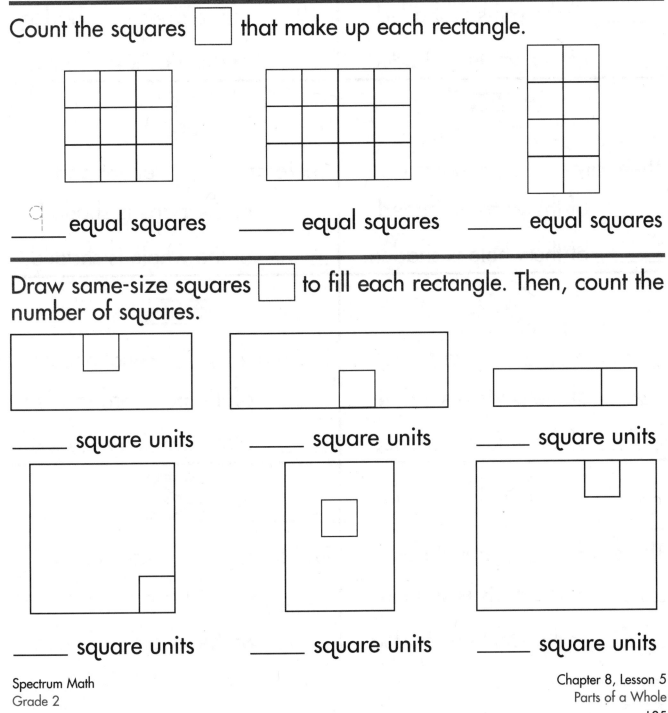

_9_ equal squares   ____ equal squares   ____ equal squares

Draw same-size squares ▢ to fill each rectangle. Then, count the number of squares.

____ square units   ____ square units   ____ square units

____ square units   ____ square units   ____ square units

Check What You Learned

Parts of a Whole

There are _____ equal parts.

_____ of the parts is shaded.

_____ of the whole is shaded.

There are _____ equal parts.

_____ of the parts are shaded.

_____ of the whole is shaded.

There are _____ equal parts.

_____ of the parts is shaded.

_____ of the whole is shaded.

There are _____ equal parts.

_____ of the parts is shaded.

_____ of the whole is shaded.

There are _____ equal parts.

_____ of the parts is shaded.

_____ of the whole is shaded.

There are _____ equal parts.

_____ of the parts are shaded.

_____ of the whole is shaded.

There are _____ equal parts.

_____ of the parts is shaded.

_____ of the whole is shaded.

There are _____ equal parts.

_____ of the parts are shaded.

_____ of the whole is shaded.

Check What You Learned

Parts of a Whole

Write the fraction shown. Use numbers. Then, use words.

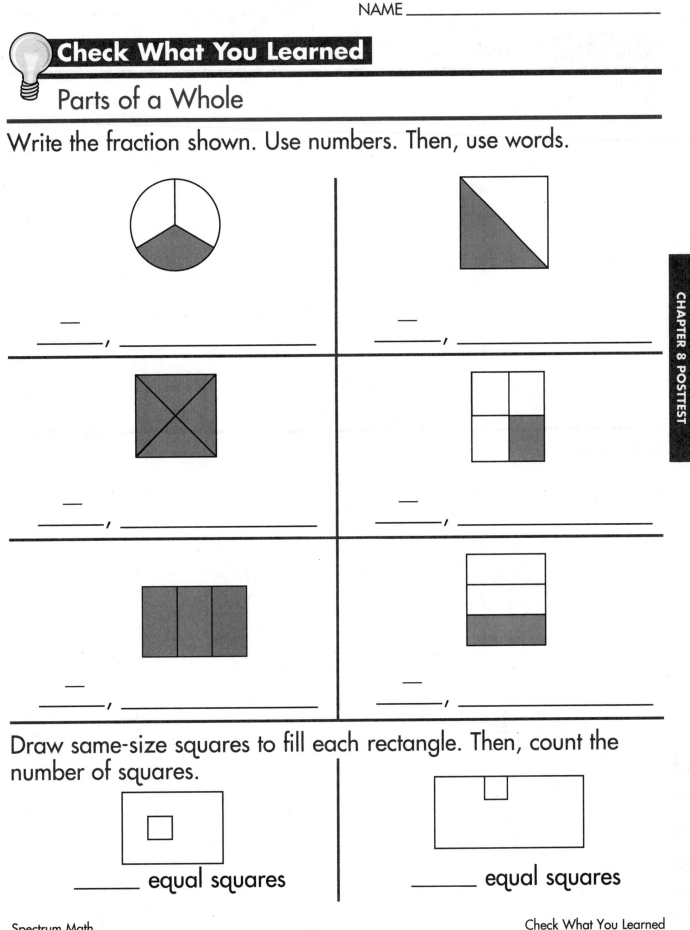

_____
_____ , _____

_____
_____ , _____

_____
_____ , _____

_____
_____ , _____

_____
_____ , _____

_____
_____ , _____

Draw same-size squares to fill each rectangle. Then, count the number of squares.

_____ equal squares

_____ equal squares

Final Test Chapters 1–8

Add.

9 +8	26 +34	7 +3	42 +17	7 +6	33 +45

					16
23 +16	5 +0	47 + 9	74 +17	8 +7	20 +32

293 + 418	502 + 334	165 + 775	635 + 206	747 + 207	456 + 299

Subtract.

79 −36	15 − 9	75 −36	7 −7	68 −22	17 − 8

11 − 3	82 −79	4 −3	50 −23	9 −5	78 −55

881 − 17	803 − 29	746 − 48	202 − 96	236 − 48	318 − 45

802 − 359	438 − 118	877 − 335	602 − 420	930 − 115	738 − 309

Final Test Chapters 1–8

Count how many. Write the number word. Write odd or even.

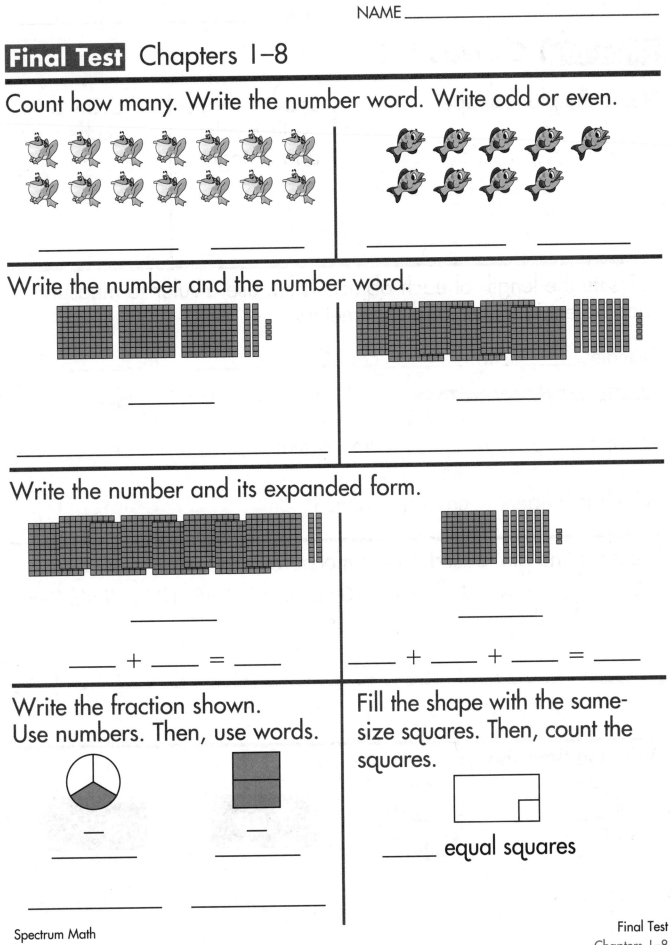

_____   _____

_____   _____

Write the number and the number word.

_____

_____   _____

Write the number and its expanded form.

_____

____ + ____ = ____

_____

____ + ____ + ____ = ____

Write the fraction shown.
Use numbers. Then, use words.

____

_____

____

_____

Fill the shape with the same-size squares. Then, count the squares.

____ equal squares

Spectrum Math
Grade 2

Final Test
Chapters 1–8
139

CHAPTERS 1–8 FINAL TEST

NAME _____

Final Test Chapters 1–8

Name the plane shape.

_____   _____

Draw a shape with 3 sides and 3 angles.	Draw a cube.

Estimate the length of each object. Then, use a ruler to measure each object in inches and centimeters.

Estimate: _____ in. _____ cm   Estimate: _____ in. _____ cm

Actual: _____ in. _____ cm   Actual: _____ in. _____ cm

Which is longer?   crayon   pencil

Create a line plot based on the measurements below.

12 in., 9 in., 12 in., 2 in., 4 in., 10 in., 3 in., 11 in., 10 in., 4 in., 9 in.

Write the time shown.

_____ : _____   _____ : _____

7:00	3:45
_____ o'clock	_____ forty-five

Final Test Chapters 1–8

Callie asked her classmates about their favorite drinks. She made this picture graph with the results.

Our Favorite Drinks

Milk	🥛 🥛 🥛 🥛
Apple Juice	🥛 🥛 🥛 🥛
Grape Juice	🥛 🥛 🥛
Other	🥛 🥛 🥛

🥛 = 2 students

Use the graph to answer these questions.

How many students does each glass represent? _____

How many students chose grape juice? _____

Which drink did most students choose? _____

Use the information in the tally chart to complete the bar graph.

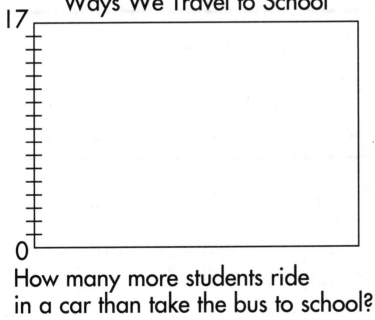

Ways We Travel to School

17

0

Ways We Travel to School	
Bus	I I I I
Walk	⊬⊬⊬⊬ ⊬⊬⊬⊬
Car	⊬⊬⊬⊬ ⊬⊬⊬⊬ I
Bike	I I

How many more students ride
in a car than take the bus to school? _____

Spectrum Math
Grade 2

Final Test
Chapters 1–8
141

CHAPTERS 1–8 FINAL TEST

Final Test Chapters 1–8

NAME _____

Solve each problem.

Jenny is reading a book that is 98 pages long.
She has read 47 pages so far.
How many pages does Jenny have left to read? _____

47 + _____ = 98

Addison bakes 14 loaves of bread.
After she gives some away, she has 6 left.
How many loaves of bread does Addison have left? _____

14 – _____ = 6

Courtney had some fabric.
Becca gave her 12 more feet of fabric.
Now Courtney has 65 feet of fabric.
How many feet of fabric did Courtney have to start with? _____

_____ + 12 = 65

There are 12 campers in the lake for an afternoon swim.
6 more campers join them.
If 9 of the campers get out of the lake,
how many campers are left swimming in the lake? _____

Kayla rakes 14 piles of leaves in her front yard.
She rakes 15 piles of leaves in her back yard.
Then, she rakes 10 piles of leaves in her neighbor's yard.
How many piles of leaves does Kayla rake in all? _____

Final Test Chapters 1-8

Solve each problem.

Denise has 2 nickels and 2 pennies.
How much money does Denise have? _____

Colby has 2 quarters in his pocket.
Nikki gives Colby 5 pennies that she found on the floor.
How much money does Colby have now? _____

Connor has 11 centimeters of green string and
19 centimeters of purple string to put on his birthday balloons.
How much total string does Conner have for the balloons?

_____

Mrs. Shaw bought 27 yards of fabric to make curtains for her
classroom. Ms. Wolf bought 36 yards of fabric to make curtains
for her classroom.
How much more fabric did Ms. Wolf buy than Mrs. Shaw?

_____

Vanessa's yo-yo string measures 32 inches.
Tony's yo-yo string measures 32 inches.
How many inches of yo-yo string do Vanessa
and Tony have altogether?

_____

Spectrum Math
Grade 2

Final Test
Chapters 1-8
143

CHAPTERS 1-8 FINAL TEST

NAME _____ DATE _____

Scoring Record for Posttests, Mid-Test, and Final Test

Chapter Posttest	Your Score	Performance			
		Excellent	Very Good	Fair	Needs Improvement
1	____ of 31	28–31	25–27	22–24	21 or fewer
2	____ of 41	39–41	34–38	26–33	25 or fewer
3	____ of 41	39–41	34–38	26–33	25 or fewer
4	____ of 35	32–34	28–31	25–27	24 or fewer
5	____ of 62	56–62	50–55	44–49	45 or fewer
6	____ of 20	18–19	16–17	14–15	13 or fewer
7	____ of 22	20–22	18–19	15–17	14 or fewer
8	____ of 38	35–38	31–34	23–30	22 or fewer
Mid-Test	____ of 65	59–65	52–58	46–53	45 or fewer
Final Test	____ of 93	84–92	75–83	66–74	65 or fewer

Record your test score in the Your Score column. See where your score falls in the Performance columns. Your score is based on the total number of required responses. If your score is fair or needs improvement, review the chapter material.

Grade 2 Answers

Chapter 1

Pretest, page 5
Even; odd
odd; even
4 + 4 + 4 = 12; 5 + 5 = 10

Pretest, page 6
4 + 4 + 4 + 4 = 16; 1 + 1 + 1 = 3
20, 30, 50, 60
10, 20, 25, 30
24, 26, 30, 32, 34

Lesson 1.1, page 7
3 + 3 = 6; 5 + 5 + 5 + 5 = 20
4 + 4 + 4 = 12; 1 + 1 + 1 + 1 + 1 = 5
3 + 3 + 3 = 9; 4 + 4 = 8

Lesson 1.1, page 8
2 + 2 = 4; 4 + 4 + 4 + 4 = 16
1 + 1 = 2; 5 + 5 + 5 = 15
5 + 5 + 5 + 5 + 5 = 25; 5 + 5 = 10

Lesson 1.2, page 9
8, 14
15, 20, 30, 35
40, 50, 60
14, 16, 22
20, 30, 35, 55, 65, 75, 80
80, 60, 40, 30

Lesson 1.3, page 10
8, 10, 12
84, 88, 90
10, 20, 30

Lesson 1.3, page 11
55, 65, 75
20, 40, 50, 80, 90
80, 60, 40, 30, 20

Lesson 1.4, page 12
8, even, 4 + 4 = 8; 5, odd

Lesson 1.4, page 13

8, 4 + 4 = 8, even; 3, odd
7, odd; 6, 3 + 3 = 6, even

Posttest, page 14
4, 6, 10, 12
10, 15, 25, 30
40, 50, 60, 90
5 + 5 + 5 + 5 + 5 = 25; 3 + 3 = 6

Posttest, page 15
5 + 5 + 5 + 5 = 20; 5 + 5 + 5 = 15
9, odd; 10, even, 5 + 5 = 10
1, odd; 5, odd
6, even, 3 + 3 = 6; 4, even, 2 + 2 = 4

Chapter 2

Pretest, page 16
16, 5, 2, 11, 7, 15
8, 19, 12, 4, 9, 17
3, 6, 13, 14, 20, 10
1, 7, 2, 5, 8, 9
7, 12, 3, 0, 8, 6
9, 3, 3, 17, 8, 5

Pretest, page 17

$$\begin{array}{r} 6 \\ +8 \\ \hline 14 \end{array}$$

$$\begin{array}{r} 17 \\ -\ 8 \\ \hline 9 \end{array}$$

$$\begin{array}{r} 20 \\ -\ 6 \\ \hline 14 \end{array}$$

$$\begin{array}{r} 6 \\ +\ 2 \\ \hline 8 \end{array}$$

$$\begin{array}{r} 8 \\ +\ 7 \\ \hline 15 \end{array}$$

Lesson 2.1, page 18
5, 4, 5, 4, 1, 3
2, 2, 5, 3, 4, 3
4, 0, 5, 4, 4, 2
1, 5, 3, 4, 5, 2
0, 2 ,5, 3, 4, 5

Grade 2 Answers

Lesson 2.2, page 19
3, 0, 0, 1, 3, 3
0, 1, 0, 1, 2, 4
4, 2, 2, 0, 2, 3
1, 5, 0, 3, 0, 0
1, 3, 1, 2, 3, 4

Lesson 2.3, page 20
6, 8, 7, 7, 8, 8
6, 6, 7, 6, 8, 8
7, 7, 8, 7, 6, 6
8, 8, 7, 8, 6, 7
8, 8, 7, 6, 6, 7

Lesson 2.4, page 21
4, 6, 3, 4, 3, 4
7, 1, 2, 0, 5, 0
5, 6, 3, 1, 2, 2
0, 6, 5, 7, 8, 1
4, 5, 4, 4, 0, 3

Lesson 2.5, page 22
9, 10, 10, 9, 10, 9
9, 9, 10, 10, 10, 9
9, 9, 9, 9, 9, 10
9, 10, 10, 10, 9, 9
9, 10, 10, 10, 10, 9

Lesson 2.6, page 23
3, 5, 6, 6, 1, 2
9, 1, 4, 2, 8, 4
9, 5, 3, 7, 7, 10
0, 8, 6, 1, 9, 4
1, 5, 8, 2, 2, 7

Lesson 2.7, page 24
12, 11, 13, 11, 12, 11
12, 13, 12, 12, 11, 13
11, 12, 11, 13, 11, 13
13, 11, 12, 12, 13, 11
11, 12, 12, 13, 13, 11

Lesson 2.8, page 25
8, 2, 4, 7, 9, 5
3, 7, 5, 9, 6, 6
9, 4, 3, 8, 6, 8
7, 8, 4, 6, 7, 4
9, 7, 3, 9, 5, 5

Lesson 2.9, page 26
14, 12, 16, 13, 14, 11
11, 14, 13, 16, 12, 16
14, 15, 12, 11, 14, 13
15, 12, 12, 11, 15, 15
13, 14, 11, 16, 11, 14

Lesson 2.10, page 27
5, 7, 5, 8, 7, 4
5, 9, 6, 7, 9, 6
9, 7, 8, 2, 6, 8
4, 3, 6, 8, 9, 9
7, 7, 5, 8, 5, 7

Lesson 2.11, page 28
18, 17, 16, 13, 19, 12
14, 20, 15, 12, 15, 17
17, 14, 12, 13, 12, 14
19, 13, 18, 15, 12, 20
20, 14, 13, 17, 16, 19

Lesson 2.12, page 29
9, 8, 6, 8, 6, 11
3, 9, 8, 5, 7, 6
8, 6, 8, 12, 5, 9
8, 9, 5, 4, 16, 7
15, 9, 9, 4, 7, 10

Lesson 2.13, page 30

$$
\begin{array}{r} 13 \\ -\ 7 \\ \hline 6 \end{array}
$$

$$
\begin{array}{r} 8 \\ +\ 6 \\ \hline 14 \end{array}
$$

$$
\begin{array}{r} 15 \\ -\ 7 \\ \hline 8 \end{array}
$$

$$
\begin{array}{r} 6 \\ +\ ③ \\ \hline 9 \end{array}
$$

$$
\begin{array}{r} 18 \\ -\ 9 \\ \hline 9 \end{array}
$$

Grade 2 Answers

Lesson 2.13, page 31

subtract; 12
$$\begin{array}{r} 12 \\ -6 \\ \hline 6 \end{array}$$

subtract; 20
$$\begin{array}{r} 20 \\ -5 \\ \hline 15 \end{array}$$

add; 6
$$\begin{array}{r} 6 \\ +7 \\ \hline 13 \end{array}$$

$$\begin{array}{r} 9 \\ -5 \\ \hline 4 \end{array}$$

Posttest, page 32

7, 10, 12, 3, 16, 18
9, 13, 6, 4, 14, 5
8, 20, 15, 17, 11, 19
9, 6, 2, 6, 1, 5
10, 9, 0, 9, 6, 6
8, 9, 16, 0, 3, 0

Posttest, page 33

$$\begin{array}{r} 15 \\ -6 \\ \hline 9 \end{array}$$

$$\begin{array}{r} 7 \\ +5 \\ \hline 12 \end{array}$$

$$\begin{array}{r} 12 \\ -5 \\ \hline 7 \end{array}$$

$$\begin{array}{r} 9 \\ +9 \\ \hline 18 \end{array}$$

$$\begin{array}{r} 19 \\ -3 \\ \hline 16 \end{array}$$

Chapter 3

Pretest, page 34

57, 74, 98, 59, 69
59, 91, 39, 58, 93
39, 68, 78, 96, 59
5, 27, 20, 13, 22
24, 27, 50, 17, 3
35, 31, 6, 20, 22

Pretest, page 35

$$\begin{array}{r} 46 \\ -22 \\ \hline 24 \end{array}$$

$$\begin{array}{r} 36 \\ +22 \\ \hline 58 \end{array}$$

$$\begin{array}{r} 37 \\ -25 \\ \hline 12 \end{array}$$

$$\begin{array}{r} 58 \\ -45 \\ \hline 13 \end{array}$$

$$\begin{array}{r} 53\cent \\ -41\cent \\ \hline 12\cent \end{array}$$

Lesson 3.1, page 36

64, 79, 79, 87, 74
76, 48, 87, 94, 88
91, 89, 98, 69, 89
87, 69, 85, 79, 59
95, 77, 98, 59, 53

Lesson 3.1, page 37

69, 97, 39, 79, 75
99, 79, 39, 57, 86
56, 88, 49, 67, 68
49, 68, 63, 76, 89
56, 69, 56, 48, 99
94, 76, 78, 58, 77
78, 89, 78, 98, 63

Lesson 3.2, page 38

67, 89, 85, 79, 39
69, 84, 77, 47, 87
89, 57, 89, 96, 69
85, 27, 94, 89, 40
96, 77, 67, 84, 65
69, 94, 86, 67, 87
49, 39, 54, 87, 77

Grade 2 Answers

Lesson 3.2, page 39

$$\begin{array}{r} 10 \\ +11 \\ \hline 21 \end{array}$$

$$\begin{array}{r} 42 \\ +33 \\ \hline 75 \end{array}$$

$$\begin{array}{r} 13 \\ +20 \\ \hline 33 \end{array}$$

$$\begin{array}{r} 28 \\ -14 \\ \hline 14 \end{array}$$

$$\begin{array}{r} 32 \\ +27 \\ \hline 59 \end{array}$$

Lesson 3.3, page 40

10, 81, 12, 14, 52
16, 53, 30, 12, 15
21, 14, 33, 24, 26
11, 30, 60, 31, 22
5, 14, 10, 62, 5

Lesson 3.3, page 41

11, 23, 25, 50, 14
13, 26, 21, 33, 31
52, 24, 11, 35, 20
33, 42, 17, 10, 24
91, 14, 4, 31, 12
14, 90, 34, 32, 41
25, 61, 62, 13, 11

Lesson 3.4, page 42

22, 34, 10, 16, 6
72, 18, 3, 60, 45
25, 32, 43, 45, 1
35, 43, 54, 40, 21
15, 32, 51, 40, 13
80, 60, 14, 74, 21
43, 20, 26, 18, 22

Lesson 3.4, page 43

$$\begin{array}{r} 28 \\ -10 \\ \hline 18 \end{array}$$

$$\begin{array}{r} 32 \\ -30 \\ \hline 2 \end{array}$$

$$\begin{array}{r} 65 \\ -22 \\ \hline 43 \end{array}$$

$$\begin{array}{r} 59 \\ -44 \\ \hline 15 \end{array}$$

$$\begin{array}{r} 37 \\ -12 \\ \hline 25 \end{array}$$

Lesson 3.5, page 44

69, 88, 87, 68, 96
87, 49, 87, 65, 59
69, 56, 58, 47, 66
79, 39, 77, 68, 88

Lesson 3.5, page 45

$$\begin{array}{r} 10 \\ 12 \\ +25 \\ \hline 47 \end{array}$$

$$\begin{array}{r} 14 \\ 15 \\ +20 \\ \hline 49 \end{array}$$

$$\begin{array}{r} 6 \\ 22 \\ +30 \\ \hline 58 \end{array}$$

$$\begin{array}{r} 32 \\ 26 \\ +10 \\ \hline 68 \end{array}$$

$$\begin{array}{r} 14 \\ 23 \\ +30 \\ \hline 67 \end{array}$$

Grade 2 Answers

Lesson 3.6, page 46

30¢　　32¢　　(42¢)　　24¢

$$\begin{array}{r} 30¢ \\ +42¢ \\ \hline 72¢ \end{array} \qquad \begin{array}{r} 32¢ \\ +24¢ \\ \hline 56¢ \end{array}$$

$$\begin{array}{r} 30¢ \\ +32¢ \\ \hline 62¢ \end{array} \qquad \begin{array}{r} 42¢ \\ +24¢ \\ \hline 66¢ \end{array}$$

$$\begin{array}{r} 30¢ \\ 42¢ \\ +24¢ \\ \hline 96¢ \end{array} \qquad \begin{array}{r} 32¢ \\ 24¢ \\ +30¢ \\ \hline 86¢ \end{array}$$

Lesson 3.6, page 47

melon
apple

$$\begin{array}{r} 85¢ \\ -33¢ \\ \hline 52¢ \end{array} \qquad \begin{array}{r} 33¢ \\ -20¢ \\ \hline 13¢ \end{array}$$

$$\begin{array}{r} 35¢ \\ -20¢ \\ \hline 15¢ \end{array} \qquad \begin{array}{r} 85¢ \\ -20¢ \\ \hline 65¢ \end{array}$$

$$\begin{array}{r} 85¢ \\ -35¢ \\ \hline 50¢ \end{array} \qquad \begin{array}{r} 35¢ \\ -33¢ \\ \hline 2¢ \end{array}$$

Posttest, page 48

79, 36, 93, 66, 57, 99
47, 28, 59, 58, 84, 35
59, 68, 27, 87, 49, 69
16, 24, 13, 41, 50, 22
53, 70, 3, 33, 34, 24
73, 10, 25, 30, 17, 44

Posttest, page 49

$$\begin{array}{r} 15 \\ +14 \\ \hline 29 \end{array}$$

$$\begin{array}{r} 27 \\ +31 \\ \hline 58 \end{array} \qquad \begin{array}{r} 58 \\ -5 \\ \hline (53) \end{array}$$

$$\begin{array}{r} 24 \\ -3 \\ \hline 21 \end{array}$$

$$\begin{array}{r} 65 \\ -45 \\ \hline 20 \end{array}$$

$$\begin{array}{r} 45¢ \\ +52¢ \\ \hline 97¢ \end{array}$$

Chapter 4

Pretest, page 50

82, 75, 63, 90, 83
73, 41, 57, 72, 95
91, 61, 84, 60, 44
28, 5, 18, 6, 38
17, 28, 48, 22, 58
24, 7, 49, 74, 27

Pretest, page 51

$$\begin{array}{r} 61 \\ -45 \\ \hline 16 \end{array}$$

$$\begin{array}{r} 38 \\ +35 \\ \hline 73 \end{array} \qquad \begin{array}{r} 73 \\ -3 \\ \hline (70) \end{array}$$

$$\begin{array}{r} 72 \\ -44 \\ \hline 28 \end{array}$$

$$\begin{array}{r} 91 \\ -45 \\ \hline 46 \end{array}$$

$$\begin{array}{r} 95 \\ -38 \\ \hline 57 \end{array}$$

Lesson 4.1, page 52

81, 92, 64, 37, 82
92, 96, 84, 81, 36
72, 62, 51, 92, 85
70, 73, 70, 30, 91

Lesson 4.1, page 53

90, 63, 70, 90, 64
50, 83, 60, 72, 42
71, 91, 80, 85, 60
55, 80, 41, 84, 70
70, 82, 61, 60, 82
73, 71, 64, 47, 81

Grade 2 Answers

Lesson 4.2, page 54
71, 51, 83, 60, 64
73, 61, 60, 75, 67
41, 82, 92, 52, 92
53, 51, 71, 40, 81
60, 82, 92, 65, 72
90, 83, 63, 84, 85

Lesson 4.2, page 55

$$\begin{array}{r} 35 \\ +39 \\ \hline 74 \end{array}$$

$$\begin{array}{r} 48 \\ +36 \\ \hline 84 \end{array} \qquad \begin{array}{r} 84 \\ -30 \\ \hline \boxed{54} \end{array}$$

$$\begin{array}{r} 33 \\ +28 \\ \hline 61 \end{array}$$

$$\begin{array}{r} 9 \\ +\boxed{15} \\ \hline 24 \end{array}$$

$$\begin{array}{r} 15 \\ +16 \\ \hline 31 \end{array}$$

Lesson 4.3, page 56
29, 12, 29, 37, 7
57, 12, 27, 9, 57
15, 37, 5, 21, 19
38, 15, 15, 28, 56

Lesson 4.3, page 57
3, 9, 18, 88, 45
13, 16, 17, 9, 36
4, 26, 29, 9, 48
16, 38, 24, 8, 16
19, 8, 37, 16, 27

Lesson 4.4, page 58
9, 17, 9, 17, 26
36, 45, 9, 28, 27
4, 28, 48, 47, 36
15, 29, 46, 26, 48
36, 37, 8, 24, 49
18, 24, 9, 35, 56

Lesson 4.4, page 59

$$\begin{array}{r} 33 \\ -28 \\ \hline 5 \end{array}$$

$$\begin{array}{r} 25 \\ +27 \\ \hline 52 \end{array} \qquad \begin{array}{r} 52 \\ -19 \\ \hline \boxed{33} \end{array}$$

$$\begin{array}{r} 31 \\ -8 \\ \hline 23 \end{array}$$

$$\begin{array}{r} 26 \\ -\boxed{8} \\ \hline 18 \end{array}$$

$$\begin{array}{r} 42 \\ -27 \\ \hline 15 \end{array}$$

Posttest, page 60
60, 84, 92, 73, 42
63, 80, 53, 72, 63
53, 50, 83, 60, 24
39, 9, 35, 6, 26
18, 6, 29, 38, 8
38, 26, 47, 9, 15

Posttest, page 61

$$\begin{array}{r} 50 \\ +38 \\ \hline 88 \end{array} \qquad \begin{array}{r} 88 \\ -10 \\ \hline \boxed{78} \end{array}$$

$$\begin{array}{r} 57 \\ +39 \\ \hline 96 \end{array}$$

$$\begin{array}{r} 60 \\ -51 \\ \hline 9 \end{array}$$

$$\begin{array}{r} 42 \\ -18 \\ \hline 24 \end{array}$$

$$\begin{array}{r} 37 \\ +29 \\ \hline 66 \end{array}$$

Grade 2 Answers

Mid-Test

Page 62
13, 43, 49, 14, 94, 9
17, 78, 81, 5, 69, 8
39, 78, 4, 12, 52, 68
36, 5, 9, 28, 9, 53
11, 7, 7, 10, 3, 37
8, 0, 12, 37, 8, 5

Page 63
Odd; even
50, 55, 65
14, 16, 20, 22
$4 + 4 + 4 = 12$; $5 + 5 = 10$

Page 64
$5 + 5 + 5 = 15$
50, 60, 70, 100, 110, 120, 130
14, even
$7 + 7 = 14$

$$\begin{array}{r} 14 \\ +13 \\ \hline 27 \end{array}$$

$$\begin{array}{r} 34 \\ -9 \\ \hline 25 \end{array}$$

Page 65

$$\begin{array}{r} \boxed{15} \\ -3 \\ \hline 12 \end{array}$$

$$\begin{array}{r} 24 \\ 22 \\ +21 \\ \hline 67 \end{array}$$

$$\begin{array}{r} 30¢ \\ +33¢ \\ \hline 63¢ \end{array}$$

$$\begin{array}{r} 14 \\ +18 \\ \hline 32 \end{array}$$

$$\begin{array}{r} 24 \\ +13 \\ \hline 37 \end{array} \qquad \begin{array}{r} 45 \\ -37 \\ \hline \boxed{8} \end{array}$$

Chapter 5

Pretest, page 66
455, 460, 475, 485
370, 380, 410, 420
100, 300, 400, 600, 700
234, $200 + 30 + 4 = 234$; 306, three hundred six;
$460 > 540$; $918 > 908$; $103 < 120$
$575 < 590$; $260 > 240$; $347 > 298$
$701 < 707$; $647 < 742$; $818 = 818$
$157 > 120$; $450 > 370$; $963 < 993$

Pretest, page 67
70; 178; 182; 95; 199; 283;
792; 979; 420; 905; 369; 160;
228; 277; 208; 169; 77; 417
108; 64; 510; 16; 94; 639;
444; 442; 848; 600; 732; 40;
35; 52; 37; 61; 609; 426

Lesson 5.1, page 68
165, $100 + 60 + 5$; 178, $100 + 70 + 8$
184, $100 + 80 + 4$; 158, $100 + 50 + 8$
170, $100 + 70$; 152, $100 + 50 + 2$
180, $100 + 80$; 161, $100 + 60 + 1$

Lesson 5.2, page 69
235, two hundred thirty five; 309, three hundred nine
324, three hundred twenty four; 217,
    two hundred seventeen
390, three hundred ninety; 289, two hundred eighty nine
241, two hundred forty one; 307, three hundred seven

Lesson 5.3, page 70
542, five hundred forty two; 435, four hundred thirty five
640, six hundred forty; 514, five hundred fourteen
494, four hundred ninety four; 671,
six hundred seventy one
433, four hundred thirty three; 508, five hundred eight

Lesson 5.4, page 71
722, $700 + 20 + 2$
956, $900 + 50 + 6$; 809, $800 + 9$
840, $800 + 40$
774, $700 + 70 + 4$; 963, $900 + 60 + 3$
917, $900 + 10 + 7$

Grade 2 Answers

Lesson 5.5, page 72
313, 315, 316
417, 419, 421
610, 615, 620, 635
785, 795, 810 ,815
210, 220, 240, 260
360, 380, 390, 410, 420
200, 400, 500, 700
700, 600, 400, 300

Lesson 5.6, page 73
410, 415, 420, 435, 440
320, 330, 340, 370
660, 650, 640, 610
502, 492, 472, 462
440, 540, 740, 840
210, 310, 510, 610, 710
850, 750, 650, 550, 350
726, 626, 426, 326

Lesson 5.6, page 74
831 < 843; 436 > 379; 902 < 911
567 > 564; 306 < 401; 535 = 535
219 > 198; 739 > 730; 630 < 820
127 > 119; 407 < 610; 923 < 925
354 < 453; 802 > 792; 236 < 401
504 = 504; 402 < 408; 123 > 118
367 < 562; 760 > 740; 654 < 736
981 > 901; 391 < 491; 835 > 830

Lesson 5.6, page 75
122 < 245; 903 > 500; 418 < 806
856 > 424; 806 > 751; 980 > 361
744 > 121; 168 < 388; 959 > 767
676 < 806; 371 < 638; 492 < 746
861 > 445; 775 > 134; 393 > 296
433 < 816; 189 = 189; 101 < 788;
689 > 341; 365 < 815; 483 < 504;
770 > 310; 379 < 462; 403 < 404;
510 = 510; 506 < 736; 311 < 482;
646 < 740; 673 > 355; 180 < 483;
148 < 569; 823 > 511; 568 = 568;
639 < 660; 938 > 302; 764 > 741

Lesson 5.7, page 76
140; 61; 151; 111; 94
81; 110; 104; 111; 121
141; 44; 120; 93; 91
81; 134; 121; 94; 62
43; 101; 80; 141; 127
114; 122; 120; 94; 88

Lesson 5.7, page 77
89; 78; 88; 86; 77
79; 79; 67; 66; 68
26; 8; 48; 89; 69
78; 58; 69; 86; 59
28; 58; 29; 58; 74
85; 69; 79; 75; 87

Lesson 5.7, page 78
61; 109; 106; 92; 90
55; 71; 84; 59; 117;
80; 70; 105; 47; 74
91; 91; 97; 66; 72
91; 67; 129; 85
87; 89; 101; 98; 71

Lesson 5.7, page 79
58; 91; 116; 82; 79;
84; 64; 122; 115; 124;
7; 78; 78; 49; 91;
589; 377; 590; 767; 851
773; 703; 386; 617; 658
434; 691; 790; 488; 43

Lesson 5.8, page 80
685; 1,153; 933; 1,123; 444
1,175; 1,030; 1,570; 1,042; 1,280
1,282; 1,001; 681; 973; 1,356
982; 944; 367; 404; 414
1,424; 850; 1,378; 1,350; 446
1,334; 1,070; 880; 1,251; 1,125

Lesson 5.9, page 81
212; 593; 489; 120; 480
408; 206; 279; 106; 377
331; 399; 519; 189; 577
114; 208; 529; 171; 448
86; 627; 25; 350; 86
281; 349; 225; 336; 129

Lesson 5.10, page 82
369; 901; 417; 732; 521
1,108; 606; 1,075; 1,005; 397
847; 711; 931; 550; 531
1,055; 589; 812; 902; 382

Lesson 5.11, page 83
570; 238; 33; 326; 165;
121; 15; 226; 112; 129;
399; 220; 106; 263; 264
187; 462; 437; 303; 215

Grade 2 Answers

Lesson 5.12, page 84

131; 179; 91; 94; 422
268; 62; 337; 60; 779;
447; 77; 89; 175; 198
1,403; 313; 860; 79; 465
905; 365; 370; 198; 204
223; 922; 689; 396; 302

Lesson 5.12, page 85

75; 119; 120; 649; 905
106; 585; 349; 91; 402
1,344; 118; 390; 580; 149
54; 72; 339; 344; 861
121; 916; 435; 688; 478
14; 510; 651; 681; 777

Lesson 5.12, page 86

131; 158; 86; 117; 664
401; 162; 520; 140; 197;
1,111; 164; 620; 999; 329
397; 108; 183; 409; 889
88; 147; 591; 430; 406
306; 463; 378; 106; 403

Posttest, page 87

110, 115, 125, 130
660, 680, 690, 710
475, 675, 775, 875
550, 500 + 50
129, 100 + 20 +9
218, two hundred eighteen
163, one hundred sixty-three
410 < 501; 653 < 672; 946 > 942
378 > 350; 741 > 561; 143 < 206

Posttest, page 88

167; 345; 249; 402; 922; 868
279; 375; 1,750; 345; 1,273; 360
969; 407; 856; 1,042; 915; 990
137; 106; 78; 40; 270; 186
288; 617; 231; 115; 394; 364
159; 477; 187; 683; 485; 169

Chapter 6

Pretest, page 89

Check student's estimates against actual lengths, 3.5 in.,
9 cm; Check student's estimates against actual lengths,
2 in., 4.5 cm
pencil; centimeters; an inch

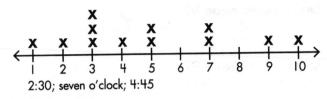

2:30; seven o'clock; 4:45

Pretest, page 90

Cookie dough; 7; 12
75; 60

Pretest, page 91

$$\begin{array}{r} 98 \text{ in.} \\ -95 \text{ in.} \\ \hline 3 \text{ in.} \end{array}$$

$$\begin{array}{r} 5¢ \\ +7¢ \\ \hline 12¢ \end{array}$$

$$\begin{array}{r} 5 \text{ in.} \\ + 7 \text{ in.} \\ \hline 12 \text{ in.} \end{array}$$

$$\begin{array}{r} \$4.05 \\ -\$2.00 \\ \hline \$2.05 \end{array}$$

$$\begin{array}{r} 60 \text{ in.} \\ -51 \text{ in.} \\ \hline 9 \text{ in.} \end{array}$$

Lesson 6.1, page 92

7, 7:00; 12, 12:00; 11, 11:00
10, 10:00; 6, 6:00; 5, 5:00
9, 9:00; 8, 8:00; 2, 2:00

Lesson 6.2, page 93

4, 4:30; 10, 10:30; 11, 11:30
2, 2:30; 1, 1:30; 6, 6:30
5, 5:30; 9, 9:30; 3, 3:30

Lesson 6.3, page 94

6:45; 5:15; 10:15
3:45; 11:15; 7:45

Lesson 6.3, page 95

3, 4; 6; 3:30
5, 6; 9; 5:45
8; 12; 8:00
10, 11; 3; 10:15
4; 12; 4:00

Grade 2 Answers

Lesson 6.4, page 96
Check student's estimates against actual lengths: 5 in., 4 in., 2 in., 7 in., 3 in.

Lesson 6.5, page 97
Check student's estimates against actual lengths: 6 cm, 5 cm, 9 cm, 12 cm, 9 cm

Lesson 6.6, page 98
3 in.
5 in.
3 in.; 2 in.
6 in.
1 in.; 3 in.

Lesson 6.7, page 99
1; 1; 2; 0; 1; 1

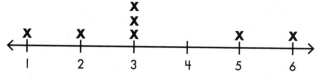

Lesson 6.8, page 100
1 in.; 5 in.
2 in.; 4 in.
3, 1, 3, 1, 8 in.; 2, 2, 2, 6 in.
1, 1, 1, 1, 4 in.; 2, 1, 2, 1, 6 in.

Lesson 6.9, page 101

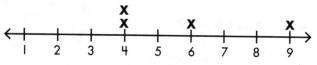

Lesson 6.10, page 102
6 cm
8 cm; 4 cm; 9 cm
7 cm
17 cm

Lesson 6.11, page 103

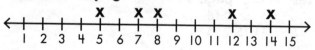

Lesson 6.12, page 104
6 cm; 5 cm
2 cm; 9 cm
6, 2, 6, 2, 16 cm; 6, 1, 6, 1, 14 cm
4, 4, 4, 4, 16 cm; 3, 3, 3, 3, 3, 15 cm

Lesson 6.13, page 105

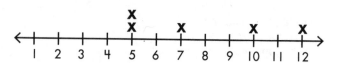

Lesson 6.14, page 106
3 in., 2 in., 1 in. longer
5 in., 3 in., 2 in. longer
1 in., 2 in., 1 in. longer
3 in., 5 in., 2 in. longer

Lesson 6.15, page 107
6 cm, 4 cm, 2 cm longer
8 cm, 4 cm, 4 cm longer
4 cm, 5 cm, 1 cm longer
7 cm, 6 cm, 1 cm longer

Lesson 6.16, page 108
11 centimeters, 22 squares
14 centimeters, 28 squares
7 centimeters, 14 squares
15 centimeters, 30 squares
Answers may vary, but students should understand that the measurements in centimeters have lower numbers than those in squares.
Answers may vary, but students should understand that the squares are smaller units than centimeters.

Lesson 6.16, page 109
2 centimeters, about 1 inch
5 centimeters, about 2 inches
10 centimeters, about 4 inches
8 centimeters, about 3 inches
16 centimeters, about 6 inches
13 centimeters, about 5 inches
Answers may vary, but students should understand that the measurements in centimeters have higher numbers than those in inches.
Answers may vary, but students should understand that centimeters are smaller units than inches.

Lesson 6.17, page 110

$$\begin{array}{r} 48 \text{ ft.} \\ +21 \text{ ft.} \\ \hline 69 \text{ ft.} \end{array}$$

$$\begin{array}{r} 27 \text{ in.} \\ -11 \text{ in.} \\ \hline 16 \text{ in.} \end{array}$$

Grade 2 Answers

20 ft.
−13 ft.
 7 ft.

25 in.
−17 in.
 8 in.

70 in.
−55 in.
15 in.

Lesson 6.18, page 111
14
4
cat
7
25

Lesson 6.18, page 112
10
7
oranges
15
1
21

Lesson 6.18, page 113
40
12
Trina
11
17
5

Lesson 6.19, page 114

Points in the Basketball Game

5	
4	
3	
2	
1	
0	Cara Evan Dawn Hugo

Evan; Hugo; 13; 4

Lesson 6.20, page 115
Check student's picture graphs

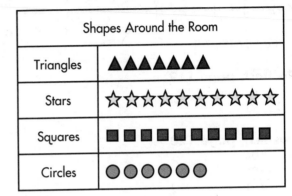

star; circle; 3; 3

Lesson 6.21, page 116
30; 35; 65; 73

Lesson 6.22, page 117
20¢
− 4¢
24¢

5¢
+7¢
12¢

10¢
− 6¢
16¢

$2.00
25¢
10¢
20¢
+ 10¢
$2.65

$1.00
50¢
40¢
5¢
+ 5¢
$2.00

Posttest, page 118
Check student's estimates against actual lengths: 6 cm, ~2.5 in.; Check student's estimates against actual lengths: 4 cm, ~1.5 in.

paper clip; centimeters; a centimeter

Grade 2 Answers

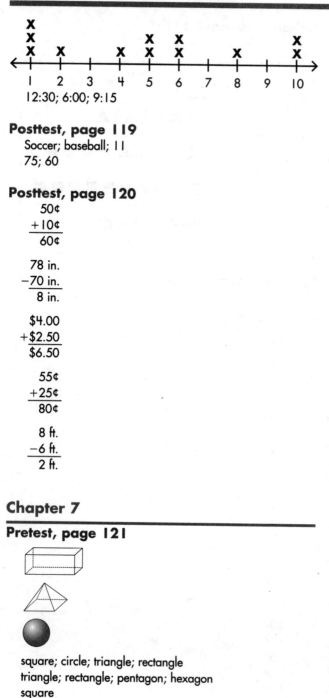

12:30; 6:00; 9:15

Posttest, page 119
Soccer; baseball; 11
75; 60

Posttest, page 120

$$\begin{array}{r} 50¢ \\ +10¢ \\ \hline 60¢ \end{array}$$

$$\begin{array}{r} 78 \text{ in.} \\ -70 \text{ in.} \\ \hline 8 \text{ in.} \end{array}$$

$$\begin{array}{r} \$4.00 \\ +\$2.50 \\ \hline \$6.50 \end{array}$$

$$\begin{array}{r} 55¢ \\ +25¢ \\ \hline 80¢ \end{array}$$

$$\begin{array}{r} 8 \text{ ft.} \\ -6 \text{ ft.} \\ \hline 2 \text{ ft.} \end{array}$$

Chapter 7

Pretest, page 121

square; circle; triangle; rectangle
triangle; rectangle; pentagon; hexagon
square
square pyramid
triangle

Pretest, page 122

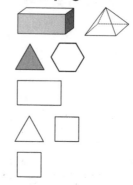

Lesson 7.1, page 123
circle; rectangle; triangle; pentagon
hexagon; square; hexagon; square
square
hexagon
circle
triangle

Lesson 7.2, page 124

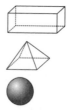

square pryamid
rectangular solid
sphere
cube

Lesson 7.3, page 125

Grade 2 Answers

Lesson 7.4, page 126
square and triangle
square
rectangle and square
circle

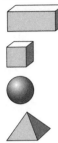

Posttest, page 127
triangle; square; rectangle; circle
pentagon; triangle; hexagon; rectangle

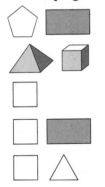

cube
rectangle
pentagon
sphere

Posttest, page 128

Chapter 8

Pretest, page 129
4, 4, $\frac{4}{4}$; 3, 1, $\frac{1}{3}$
3, 1, $\frac{1}{3}$; 2, 1, $\frac{1}{2}$
3, 3, $\frac{3}{3}$; 4, 1, $\frac{1}{4}$
4, 1, $\frac{1}{4}$; 2, 2, $\frac{2}{2}$

Pretest, page 130
$\frac{1}{3}$, one-third; $\frac{1}{4}$, one-fourth
$\frac{2}{2}$, two-halves; $\frac{1}{2}$; one-half
$\frac{1}{4}$, one-fourth; $\frac{3}{3}$; three-thirds
10; 9

Lesson 8.1, page 131
$\frac{3}{3}$, three-thirds; $\frac{2}{2}$, two-halves
$\frac{2}{2}$, two-halves; $\frac{3}{3}$, three-thirds
$\frac{4}{4}$, four-fourths; $\frac{4}{4}$, four-fourths

Lesson 8.2, page 132
2, 1, $\frac{1}{2}$; 2, 1, $\frac{1}{2}$
2, 1, $\frac{1}{2}$; 2, 1, $\frac{1}{2}$
One-half; One-half

Lesson 8.3, page 133
3, 1, $\frac{1}{3}$; 3, 1, $\frac{1}{3}$
3, 1, $\frac{1}{3}$; 3, 1, $\frac{1}{3}$
One-third; One-third

Lesson 8.4, page 134
4, 1, $\frac{1}{4}$; 4, 1, $\frac{1}{4}$
4, 1, $\frac{1}{4}$; 4, 1, $\frac{1}{4}$
One-fourth; One-fourth

Lesson 8.5, page 135
9; 12; 8
10; 12; 4
16; 12; 20

Posttest, page 136
4, 1, $\frac{1}{4}$; 4, 1, $\frac{1}{4}$
3, 1, $\frac{1}{3}$; 3, 1, $\frac{1}{3}$
2, 1, $\frac{1}{2}$; 3, 3, $\frac{3}{3}$
4, 1, $\frac{1}{4}$; 2, 2, $\frac{2}{2}$

Posttest, page 137
$\frac{1}{3}$, one-third; $\frac{1}{2}$, one-half
$\frac{4}{4}$, four-fourths; $\frac{1}{4}$, one-fourth
$\frac{3}{3}$, three-thirds; $\frac{1}{3}$, one-third
12; 18

Grade 2 Answers

Final Test

Page 138

17; 60; 10; 59; 13; 78
39; 5; 56; 91; 15; 68
711; 836; 940; 841; 954; 755
43; 6; 39; 0; 46; 9
8; 3; 1; 27; 4; 23
864; 774; 698; 106; 188; 273
443; 320; 542; 182; 815; 429

Page 139

Fourteen, even; nine, odd
324, three hundred twenty four;
675, six hundred seventy five
820, 800 + 20; 163, 100 + 60 + 3
$\frac{1}{3}$, one-third; $\frac{2}{2}$, two-halves; 8 equal squares

Page 140

pentagon; rectangle; △ ; ▱

Check student's estimates against actual lengths:
~3 in., 7 cm; ~2 in., 5 cm
pencil

9:15; 2:30; seven o'clock; three forty-five

Page 141

2; 6 ; milk

7 students

Page 142

$$\begin{array}{r} 47 \\ +\,\circled{51} \\ \hline 98 \end{array}$$

$$\begin{array}{r} 14 \\ -\,\circled{8} \\ \hline 6 \end{array}$$

$$\begin{array}{r} \circled{53} \\ +\,12 \\ \hline 65 \end{array}$$

$$\begin{array}{r} 12 \\ +\,6 \\ \hline 18 \end{array} \qquad \begin{array}{r} 18 \\ -\,9 \\ \hline \circled{9} \end{array}$$

$$\begin{array}{r} 15 \\ 14 \\ +\,10 \\ \hline 39 \end{array}$$

Page 143

$$\begin{array}{r} 10¢ \\ +\,2¢ \\ \hline 12¢ \end{array}$$

$$\begin{array}{r} 50¢ \\ +\,5¢ \\ \hline 55¢ \end{array}$$

$$\begin{array}{r} 11 \text{ cm} \\ +\,19 \text{ cm} \\ \hline 30 \text{ cm} \end{array}$$

$$\begin{array}{r} 36 \text{ yd.} \\ -\,27 \text{ yd.} \\ \hline 9 \text{ yd.} \end{array}$$

$$\begin{array}{r} 32 \text{ in.} \\ +\,32 \text{ in.} \\ \hline 64 \text{ in.} \end{array}$$